The Essence of Philosophy

UNC | COLLEGE OF ARTS AND SCIENCES
Germanic and Slavic Languages and Literatures

From 1949 to 2004, UNC Press and the UNC Department of Germanic & Slavic Languages and Literatures published the UNC Studies in the Germanic Languages and Literatures series. Monographs, anthologies, and critical editions in the series covered an array of topics including medieval and modern literature, theater, linguistics, philology, onomastics, and the history of ideas. Through the generous support of the National Endowment for the Humanities and the Andrew W. Mellon Foundation, books in the series have been reissued in new paperback and open access digital editions. For a complete list of books visit www.uncpress.org.

The Essence of Philosophy

BY WILHELM DILTHEY

TRANSLATED BY STEPHEN A. EMERY AND

WILLIAM T. EMERY

UNC Studies in the Germanic Languages and Literatures
Number 13

Copyright © 1954

This work is licensed under a Creative Commons CC BY-NC-ND license. To view a copy of the license, visit http://creativecommons.org/licenses.

Suggested citation: Dilthey, Wilhelm. *The Essence of Philosophy.* Translated by Stephen A. Emery and William T. Emery. Chapel Hill: University of North Carolina Press, 1954. DOI: https://doi.org/10.5149/9781469657417_Dilthey

Library of Congress Cataloging-in-Publication Data
Names: Emery, Stephen A. and Emery, William T.
Title: The essence of philosophy / by Stephen A. Emery and William T. Emery.
Other titles: University of North Carolina Studies in the Germanic Languages and Literatures ; no. 13.
Description: Chapel Hill : University of North Carolina Press, [1954] Series: University of North Carolina Studies in the Germanic Languages and Literatures.
Identifiers: LCCN 54014911 | ISBN 978-0-8078-8013-5 (pbk: alk. paper) | ISBN 978-1-4696-5741-7 (ebook)
Subjects: Philosophy.
Classification: LCC PD25 .N6 NO. 13 | DCC 100

Table of Contents

	Page
Translator's Preface	ix
Introduction	1

FIRST PART

Historical Procedure for Determining the Essence of Philosophy 7

I. Initial Account of the General Situation 7

II. Historical Derivation of the Essential Features of Philosophy from the Connection of its Systems 8

   1. The Origin of the Name in Greece, and its Meaning there 8

   2. The Forms of Modern Philosophy as they have been Expressed in the Definitions of Philosophy 14

      a) The New Concept of Metaphysics 14

      b) The New Non-metaphysical Definitions of Philosophy 18

   3. Conclusion concerning the Essence of Philosophy 24

III. The Connecting Links between Philosophy and Religion, Prose, and Poetry 27

SECOND PART

The Essence of Philosophy Understood from its Position in the World of Mind 33

I. Placement of the Functions of Philosophy in the System of Mental Life, of Society, and of History 33

   1. The Position of Philosophy in the Structure of Mental Life 33

   2. The Structure of Society and the Position of Religion, Art, and Philosophy in it 36

II. Theory of the *Weltanschauung*. Religion and Poetry in their Relations to Philosophy 39

1. The Religious *Weltanschauung* and its Relations to the Philosophical 42

2. Philosophy and the Life-View of the Poets 53

III. The Philosophical *Weltanschauung*. The Attempt to Raise the *Weltanschauung* to Universal Validity 60

1. The Structure of the Philosophical *Weltanschauung* 61

2. Types of Philosophical *Weltanschauung* 62

3. The Insolubility of the Problem. The Decline of the Power of Metaphysics 64

IV. Philosophy and Science 66

1. The Functions of Philosophy which Arise from Conceptual Activity in Cultural Life 67

2. The General Doctrine of Knowledge and Theory concerning the Particular Fields of Culture 68

3. The Philosophical Spirit in the Sciences and in Literature 72

V. The Concept of the Essence of Philosophy. A View of its History and Structure 73

Index of Persons 77

Translators' Preface

Wilhelm Dilthey (1833-1911), the great German humanist, was sensitive to many movements of nineteenth-century thought, and influenced recent trends so widely that he has remained a towering figure in Europe and is now entering Latin America. Perhaps he can best be epitomized as a thinker in whom German romanticism and Anglo-French positivism sought reconciliation, romanticism enriching positivism and positivism restraining romanticism. Dilthey has made noteworthy contributions to the history and fields of philosophy: metaphysics, epistemology, ethics, and aesthetics. He is distinguished also in such allied areas as psychology, sociology, history, literature, music, religion, and education. Here one finds studies of special problems, of historical developments, and of philosophical foundations. In twentieth-century Europe an extensive literature concerning Dilthey has grown up.

Within the past decade various works of Dilthey have been translated into French, Italian, and Spanish, but no complete work has yet appeared in English. So the present volume seems timely.

Das Wesen der Philosophie, offered here in translation, is in several respects peculiarly fitted to introduce readers of English to Dilthey. It is fairly brief; first appearing about four years before his death, it expresses matured views; although late in time, it serves in some sense as an overture to Dilthey's *opera*, announcing themes elaborated in his other works: the relations of philosophy to religion and the fine arts, the types of *Weltanschauung*, the psychological and social basis of the history of philosophy, the positivistic critique of metaphysics.

So much of Dilthey's extensive and complex thought is relevant to this monograph that an adequate essay of moderate length on its broader bearings would be most difficult to write. Fortunately it is not necessary. Professor H. A. Hodges of the University of Reading, a serious student of Dilthey for many years, has presented him in numerous articles and two books: *Wilhelm Dilthey: an Introduction* (1944) and *The Philosophy of Wilhelm Dilthey* (1952).[1] The earlier one consists of a concise survey of Dilthey's position, translations of twenty-nine

---

[1] Both are published by Routledge and Kegan Paul, Ltd., London.

short selections from the *Gesammelte Schriften* with notes on some technical terms, a long bibliography of Dilthey's own writings, the literature concerning him, and other relevant material. The later book gives a careful, documented account of Dilthey's various facets. These two volumes are invaluable both for the general student and as a basis for special studies.

Several frequent terms call for some comment. We are especially indebted to Professor Hodges for help with the first two. In the present work:

1) *Erlebnis* is usually translated (with Hodges) 'lived experience.' Dilthey means by *Erlebnis* (in the stricter sense) any cognitive, affective, or conative act or attitude which is conscious, but distinguished from the object to which it is directed, and not itself the object of any other act or attitude. *Erlebnisse* are too intimate to be focal. We do not know, feel, or will them; we know, feel, and will *through* them. Dilthey's *Erlebnis* and Samuel Alexander's 'enjoyment' are very close in meaning, but 'enjoyment' is so widely used in common parlance for an affective attitude involving pleasure, that it tends to retain misleading connotations in Alexander's special employment. Similarly, as 'feeling' so prevalently signifies an affective attitude, it is ill-suited to refer to other kinds of attitude, though it is true that in feeling-situations the attitude stands out with unusual clarity in distinction from the object. The past participle 'lived' indicates the peculiar, quasi-objective status of this experience, grammatically an object of living, really identical with it. For what is lived except life?

2) *Geisteswissenschaften* is rendered 'human studies.' (Here Professor Hodges in turn gives credit to a Reading colleague, Professor A. W. P. Wolters.) Dilthey means by *Geisteswissenschaften* those fields of investigation in which the chief aim is to understand some portion of mental life through the interpretation of its outward expressions in individual or social histories, in economic, political, or religious processes and institutions, or in the creative activities and products of the fine arts. Hence the *Geisteswissenschaften* comprise what are often called the social and humanistic studies. 'Human' is the appropriate adjective—free from the more restrictive meanings of 'humanistic' and 'humane'—to indicate the full scope of these disciplines.

3) *Zusammenhang* usually becomes 'system' in passages con-

cerning mind. Dilthey employs *Zusammenhang* in such contexts for a complex of many mental elements (cognitive, emotional, and volitional) united by real, inherent, lived connections, in contrast with the mere spatial and temporal contiguity of qualities, relations, and events in the outer world of the natural sciences. 'Unity' and 'continuum' fail to indicate the rich variety present; 'systematic continuum' is unwieldy in many passages; 'integration' and 'organization' have the prevalent process-product ambiguity; 'organic unity' has a neo-Hegelian flavor foreign to Dilthey; 'structure' is too static. So, for want of a better word, 'system' appears in these contexts with a rather wearisome frequency.

4) *Weltanschauung* is retained, as it is listed in English dictionaries, is commonly used, and has no adequate English equivalent. The reader should realize, however, that for Dilthey a *Weltanschauung* is a total attitude of thought, feeling, and will toward the whole natural, social, and religious environment.

Das Wesen der Philosophie first appeared in 1907 in a volume of essays on systematic philosophy by leading German authorities.[1] In 1924 it was included in a volume of Dilthey's collected works.[2] The 1924 edition, on which this translation is based, differs from the 1907 edition at several points, following Dilthey's marginal notations in his personal copy of the earlier volume. As these few differences are small and trivial, they have not been indicated in the English text.

Dr. Sarah Watson Emery, Professor Glenn R. Negley of Duke University, Professor Harold G. McCurdy and Dr. Ernst Morwitz of the University of North Carolina have given invaluable help in many ways. The University Research Council of the University of North Carolina has authorized a generous grant from the University Research Fund to aid publication. All of this assistance we gratefully acknowledge.

S. A. E.
W. T. E.

November, 1954

---

[1] *Systematische Philosophie.* (*Die Kultur der Gegenwart: ihre Entwicklung und ihre Ziele.* Herausgegeben von Paul Hinnenberg. Teil I, Abteilung VI.) B. G. Teubner, Berlin und Leipzig, 1907.

[2] *Wilhelm Dilthey's Gesammelte Schriften.* Band V. *Die Geistige Welt: Einleitung in die Philosophie des Lebens. Erste Hälfte: Abhandlungen zur Grundlegung der Geisteswissenschaften.* B. G. Teubner, Leipzig und Berlin, 1924.

Introduction

We customarily use the general idea, philosophy, to group certain products of mind which in the course of history have often arisen in various nations. If we then express in an abstract formula what is common to these particular products, usually called philosophy or philosophical, the concept of philosophy arises. This concept would reach its highest perfection in adequately presenting the essence of philosophy. Such a concept would express the formative law, operative in the origin of each individual philosophical system, and the genetic relations between the particular facts, falling under the law, would result from it.

A solution of this intellectual problem is possible only on the presupposition that what we call philosophy or philosophical really contains such a general property, so that one formative law operates in all these particular cases, and thus an inner unity embraces the whole philosophical field. And in every reference to the essence of philosophy this is the assumption. Here the term 'philosophy' means a general object. Behind the particular philosophical facts a systematic continuum of minds is presupposed as the unitary and necessary ground of these empirical facts, as the rule of their changes, and as the ordering principle which articulates their variety.

In this strict sense can one speak of an essence of philosophy? The possibility is by no means obvious. 'Philosophy' and 'philosophical' have so many meanings, differing with time and place, and the systems of thought to which their authors have applied these terms are so dissimilar, that different periods would seem to have attached to ever different systems the beautiful word 'philosophy,' coined by the Greeks. For some regard philosophy as laying the foundations of the particular sciences. Others extend the concept to include the task of deriving the system of these sciences from those foundations. Or philosophy is restricted to this system. Then again it is defined as the science of mind, the science of inner experience. Finally, it is regarded as wisdom concerning the conduct of life, or the science of the universally authentic values. Where is the inner bond, which ties together views so dissimilar, patterns so various—the unitary essence of philosophy? If such an essence cannot be found, then we are dealing merely with diverse activities which have appeared under changing historical conditions as cultural needs, and which bear a common designation only externally and through the historical accidents of terminology. There are philosophies, then; there is no philosophy. In that case the history of philosophy has no inner, necessary unity. It receives again and again different content and scope at the hands of the individual historians, always according to their conceptions of it in the contexts of their own systems. One historian may present this history as an advance to a deeper and deeper grounding of the particular sciences, another as the progressive reflection of the mind on itself, still another as the increasing knowledge concerning the experience or the values of life. In order to decide to what extent one may speak of an essence of philosophy, we must turn from the definitions, formulated by the individual philosophers, to the historical facts of philosophy itself. These facts provide the material for ascertaining what philosophy is. The result of this inductive procedure can then be understood more deeply in its conformity to law.

By what method can we solve the problem of determining the essence of philosophy from the historical facts? The question here concerns a more general problem of method in the human studies. The subjects of all statements in these studies are socially interrelated, individual selves. These are, first of all, single persons. Gestures, words, and acts are their manifestations. The problem of the human studies is to relive these selves and to grasp them in thought. The mental system expressed in these manifestations makes it possible to disclose in them a typically recurrent element, to bring the particular moments of life into the system of life-phases and finally into that of the self. Individuals, however, are not isolated, but interrelated in families, more complex groups, nations, eras, and finally humanity itself. The purposiveness in these several organizations makes possible the typical modes of approach in the human studies. Still, no concept exhausts the contents of these individual selves. Rather, the variety directly given in them can be only lived, understood, and described. And even their interweaving in the course of history is something unique, never wholly reducible to concepts. But the formations and combinations of the unique are not arbitrary. Each of them expresses the lived structural unity of individual and community life. Every report of the facts of a case, however simple, seeks at the same time to make them intelligible in the light of general ideas or concepts of mental activities. Every such report, on the basis of the general ideas or concepts available, completes a separate percept in a context supplied by one's own lived experience. Guided by the attainable experiences of intrinsic values, instrumental values, and purposes, every such report selectively and connectively unites separate elements in something significant and meaningful. The method of the human studies involves the perpetual reciprocity of lived experience and concept. In the reliving of individual and collective structural systems the concepts of the human studies find their fulfillment, while conversely the immediate reliving itself is raised to systematic knowledge by the universal forms of thought. When these two functions of consciousness, central in the human studies, finally coincide, then we grasp the essence of human development. This consciousness shall contain no concept which has not been formed in the whole fullness of historical reliving, nothing universal which does not express the essence of an historical reality. Nations, eras, lines of historical development: in these formations we do not choose freely but, committed as we are to reliving, we seek in them to clarify the essence of men and of races. Accordingly, to regard constructive thought in the historical world as only an instrument to portray and present the particular as such is to misunderstand completely the interest which thinking man brings to this world. Beyond all portrayal and description of the factual and particular, thought aims to secure knowledge of the essential and the necessary. It seeks to understand the structural system of individual and of social life. We win power over this social life only in so far as we grasp and use its regularity and coherence. The logical form of expression for such regularities is the proposition whose subject is general like its predicate.

Among the various general subject-concepts which aid in this task of the human studies belong such concepts as those of philosophy, art, religion, law, and economy. Their character is determined by the fact that they express not only an attitude present in many persons, hence something uniform, general, repeating itself in them, but also an inner system, in which the various persons are joined by this attitude. So the expression 'religion' signifies not only a class of similar facts, a vital relation of the self to invisible forces; it signifies also a communal system in which persons are united for religious rites, and in which they have special rôles in religious performances. Accordingly, in those individuals to whom religion, philosophy, or art is ascribed, the facts show a double relation. These individuals stand as particulars under a universal, as cases under a rule, and they are also joined according to this rule as parts in a whole. The reason for this will emerge for us later from our insight into the two-fold tendency in the formation of psychological concepts.

The function of these general concepts is very important in the human studies. For in these studies, just as in the natural sciences, we can grasp regularities only by teasing particular systems out of the tangled tissue, which the human-social-historical world presents, and then being able to show uniformities, inner structure, and development in these systems. Analysis of the empirically given, complex reality is the initial step to great discoveries in the human studies also. In this task we first encounter general ideas in which such systems, whose appearance is always characterized by common features, are juxtaposed, already detached and withdrawn from the complex reality. Within limits, when the bounds are correctly set by these ideas, the general subjects of assertion arising in this way can support a self-contained body of fruitful truths. And already at this stage terms like 'religion,' 'art,' 'philosophy,' 'science,' 'economy,' and 'law' are fashioned for what is expressed in such ideas.

Scientific thought has now for its basis the schematism already contained in these general ideas. But it must first test the correctness of this schematism. For it is dangerous for the human studies to adopt these ideas, since the discovery of uniformities and articulation depends upon whether in addition a unitary content is really expressed in each of them. Accordingly, in the formation of concepts in this field we seek to find the objective essence which earlier determined the general idea and use of the term, and by this essence to clarify the indefinite idea, and, indeed, perhaps to correct it where faulty. So this is the task which is set for us also in regard to the concept and the essence of philosophy.

But how more exactly shall we determine the method of advancing safely from the general idea and use of the term to the concept of the thing? The formation of concepts seems to fall into a vicious cycle. The concept of philosophy or art or the religious attitude or law can be found only as we derive from the groups of facts, forming one of these fields, the relations of the characteristics constituting the concept. This already presupposes a decision as to which groups of mental facts are to be called philosophy. But, nevertheless, thought could make this decision only if it already possessed sufficient criteria to assign to the facts the character of philosophy. So it seems that one must already know what philosophy is, when he starts to form this concept from facts.

To be sure, the question of method would be answered at once, if these concepts could be deduced from more general truths. Then the conclusions from the particular examples would have to serve merely as a supplement. And this has been the opinion of many philosophers, especially in the German speculative school. But as long as this school cannot agree concerning a universally valid deduction or win universal recognition for an intuition, we shall have to rest content with reasoning which moves empirically from the examples and seeks to find the unitary content, the genetic laws expressed in the phenomena of philosophy. This procedure must presuppose that behind the discovered use of the term lies a unitary content, so that thinking, when it starts out from the group of phenomena called philosophy or philosophical, does not wander fruitlessly. And the validity of this presupposition must be proved by the investigation itself. It wins from the instances called philosophy or philosophical a concept of essence, which must then make it possible to explain the assignment of these words to the instances. Now, in the sphere of such concepts as those of philosophy, religion, art, and science two starting points are always given; the similarity of the particular instances and the system in which these are united. And however the special nature of each one of these general concepts helps to differentiate method, in our case we enjoy further the peculiar advantage that philosophy itself has early risen to consciousness of its activity. So we have at hand a great variety of attempts to define the concept, as our method strives to do. They show what individual philosophers, determined by given cultural conditions and guided by their own systems, have regarded as philosophy. Hence these definitions epitomize its historical forms. They reveal the inner dialectic, in which philosophy has run through its possible positions in the system of culture. We must be able to make each of these possibilities fruitful for our definition.

The circularity, involved in the procedure of defining philosophy, is inevitable. In fact, a great uncertainty persists as to the bounds within which systems are called philosophy and works philosophical. This uncertainty can be overcome only by first establishing sound, even if inadequate, definitions and then moving on from these in other ways to further definitions which gradually exhaust the content of the concept. Therefore the method can be only this: through particular procedures, each of which in itself still fails to guarantee a universally valid and complete solution of the problem, step by step to mark off more precisely the essential features of philosophy and the extent of the instances possessing these features, and finally from the vitality of philosophy to explain why border fields remain, which prevent a clear demarcation of its scope. We must first try to ascertain a common property in those systems to which the general idea, philosophy, refers. Then the other side of the concept, the interconnection of the systems in a larger context, can be used to test the result and to complete it through a deeper insight. So here the basis is given for investigating the relation of the essential features of philosophy, thus discovered, to the structural system of the individual and of society, and for grasping philosophy as a vital individual and social function. We can thus combine these features into a concept of essence, from which we can understand the relations of the particular systems to the function of philosophy, put its systematic concepts into their places, and sharpen the blurred boundary of its scope. This is the way for our cursory survey.

First Part

HISTORICAL PROCEDURE FOR DETERMINING THE ESSENCE OF PHILOSOPHY

I. Initial Account of the General Situation

There are philosophical systems which above all others have stamped themselves on the consciousness of mankind, and in which permanent bearings have been found for discovering what philosophy is. Democritus, Plato, Aristotle, Descartes, Spinoza, Leibniz, Locke, Hume, Kant, Fichte, Hegel, and Comte have created systems of this kind. These have common features, in which thought achieves a standard for determining how far other systems also can be placed in the field of philosophy. First, features of a formal nature can be established in them. Irrespective of their subject-matter and method, in distinction from the particular sciences they are based on the whole range of the empirical consciousness—life, experience, and the sciences of experience—and seek thus to discharge their task. They have the character of universality, expressed in the urge to combine the separate, to establish connection and extend it without respect to the boundaries of the particular sciences. The other formal feature of philosophy lies in the demand for universally valid knowledge, hence the attempt to regress in proof to the ultimate basis of philosophy. But one who immerses himself in a comparative study of the classical systems of philosophy comes to see also—at first in hazy outlines—their affinity in content. The testimony of the philosophers concerning their creative activity—testimony well worth collecting—shows especially the youth of all thinkers as full of the struggle with the riddle of life and of the world, and in each of the systems this concern with the world-problem assumes importance in its own way. Moreover, the formal characteristics of the philosophers reveal their hidden relation to the innermost tendency to protect and mold personality, to achieve the sovereignty of the mind, the tendency to that intellectual quality which aims to make all activity conscious and to leave nothing behind in the darkness of mere behavior, ignorant of itself.

II. Historical Derivation of the Essential Features of Philosophy from the Connection of Its Systems

Now we begin to see a procedure which permits a deeper view into the essential connection of these features, explains the differences between the definitions of philosophy, assigns to each of these formulations its historical place, and determines more exactly the scope of the concept.

The concept of philosophy includes not only a general content, common to various instances, but also a connection of these instances, an historical continuity. The philosophers are chiefly and directly addressed to the riddle of the world and of life, and the concepts of philosophy which they form spring from this concern. Every position which the philosophical mind assumes in its further course is related to this basic question. Every vital philosophical work arises in this continuity. And the philosophical past acts in each individual thinker, so that, even where he despairs of solving the great riddle, he is determined by this past to adopt his new standpoint. Thus all positions of the philosophical consciousness, and all definitions of philosophy in which these positions win expression, form an historical continuity.

1. *The Origin of the Name in Greece, and its Meaning There*

The profoundly significant union of religion, art, and philosophy, in which the orientals lived, broke up with the Greeks into the three separate forms of creative mental activity. Their bright, self-confident spirit freed philosophy from the constraint of the religious attitude and from the visionary symbolism of philosophical and religious poems. Their power of plastic perception worked toward the separate development of these kinds of mental creation. Thus philosophy, its concept, and the expression *philosophia* arose in Greece together. Herodotus calls everyone *sophos* who distinguished himself in higher intellectual activity. He applies the term *sophistes* to Socrates, Pythagoras, and other earlier philosophers; Xenophon uses it for the nature-philosophers. In the vernacular of the age of Herodotus and Thucydides the compound word *philosophein* means principally the love and quest of wisdom in general, as the new Greek attitude of mind. For the Greek puts into this word the quest of truth for its own sake, the quest of a value independent of every practical application. Thus, in Herodotus, Croesus says to Solon (in that typical contrast of the oriental will to power and the new Greek ethos) that he has heard that Solon *philosopheōn* has wandered through many lands *theōriēs heineken*—an explanation of the "philosophizing." Thucydides then uses the same word in the Periclean Funeral Oration to express a fundamental feature of the contemporary Athenian mind. In the Socratic school, however, the word 'philosophy' was first raised to be the technical expression for a definite sphere of intellectual activity. For the tradition which ascribes this to Pythagoras probably referred something Socratic-Platonic to an earlier period. But, to be sure, the concept of philosophy in the Socratic-Platonic school has a duality, worthy of note.

According to Socrates, philosophy is not wisdom, but the love and quest of wisdom, for wisdom itself the gods have reserved to themselves. The critical consciousness, which in Socrates and more deeply in Plato is the ground of knowledge, also limits it. Following earlier suggestions, especially those of Heraclitus, Plato is the first thinker to raise the nature of philosophizing to consciousness. From the insights of his own philosophical genius he portrays the philosophical impulse and its unfolding into philosophical knowledge. All great living springs from the inspiration grounded in the higher nature of man. As we are imprisoned in the world of sense, this higher nature expresses itself in an infinite yearning. The philosophical *eros* passes from the love of beautiful forms through various stages to the knowledge of the Ideas. But even in this highest stage our knowledge remains only an hypothesis. And although this hypothetical knowledge has as its object the immutable essences exemplified in the world of change, yet it never reaches the causal nexus, extending from the highest Good to the particular things in which we view the eternal. In this great yearning, which our knowledge never satisfies, lies the starting point for an inner relation of philosophy to the religious attitude, which lives in the fullness of the divine.

The other aspect of the Socratic-Platonic concept indicates the positive rôle of philosophy. When comprehended, this aspect became even more generally influential. Philosophy means the nisus to knowledge—knowledge in its strictest form as science.

Universal validity, precision, and regress to the justificatory grounds of all assumptions were here first thrown into relief as a requirement for all knowledge. At least it succeeded in ending both the restless, chimerical play of metaphysical hypotheses and the scepticism of the Enlightenment. And, to be sure, in Socrates as well as in the first dialogues of Plato philosophical reflection was extended to the whole scope of knowledge in conscious opposition to its restriction to knowledge of actual existence. This reflection thus included the determination of values, of precepts, and of purposes. A view of remarkable profundity: philosophy is the reflective attitude which raises all human activity to consciousness and, indeed, to universally valid knowledge. It is the self-reflection of the mind in the form of conceptual thought. The conduct of the warrior, the statesman, the poet, or the religionist can be perfected only when knowledge of this conduct guides practice. And since all conduct needs a definite goal, the final goal being happiness, so knowledge of happiness, of the goals dependent on it and the means required by these, is the strongest element in us. No power of mysterious instincts and passions can prevail, if knowledge shows that they hinder happiness. Hence, only the sovereignty of knowledge can raise the individual to freedom, and society to its proper happiness. On the basis of this Socratic concept of philosophy the Socratic dialogues of Plato undertook to solve the problems of life. And yet just because life with its struggle for happiness, with the intrinsic power of the virtues, in which this happiness is realized, could not be raised to universally valid knowledge, these dialogues had to end negatively. The conflict in the Socratic school was irresolvable. With profound truth Plato's *Apology* grasps both elements in Socrates: how he labors to gain universally valid knowledge, and how ignorance is nevertheless his result. This concept of philosophy as striving to know the nature of being, values, goods, goals, virtues, and thus having as its object the true, the beautiful, and the good, is the first fruit of the reflection of philosophy on itself. Such reflection had an immeasurable influence, and contained the heart of the true concept of the essence of philosophy.

The Socratic-Platonic concept of philosophy later influenced Aristotle's division of philosophy into theoretical, productive, and practical science. Science, he held, is theoretical when its principle and goal are knowledge, productive when its principle lies in artistic capacity and its goal in an object to be produced, and practical when its principle is the will and its goal is action as such. Of course, productive science includes not only the theory of art, but all knowledge of a technical sort, which has its goal in the creation of an external object, not in the activity of the person.

But Aristotle did not really articulate his philosophy according to this division, growing out of Plato. A modified notion of it came to prevail with him: philosophy is no longer the highest ascent of personality and of human society through knowledge; philosophy seeks knowledge for its own sake. The philosophical attitude is theoretical. As changing, yet rational, reality is grounded in God's changeless and blessed thought, which has no goal or object beyond itself, so finally the highest of these changing realities, human reason, has its supreme function in the purely theoretical attitude as the most perfect and pleasant for man. But for Aristotle this attitude is philosophy, which underlies and embraces all the sciences. Philosophy creates a theory of knowledge as the basis for every kind of scientific work. Its center is then a universal science of being, "first philosophy" (for which the expression 'metaphysics' arose in the Aristotelian school). The teleological world-view, elaborated in this first philosophy, is the ultimate basis for the system of the sciences, which reaches from the knowledge of nature through the doctrine of man to the determination of the ultimate goal for individuals and for society. And now the new Aristotelian principle of final causality makes it possible to comprehend even the changing aspect of empirically given reality. Thus the new concept of philosophy arises: as the unity of the sciences it represents conceptually the objective system of reality, extending from the knowledge of God to the knowledge involved in man's establishment of goals.

The Greek subordination of the particular sciences to philosophy was reflected in the organization of their philosophical schools, which were not only centers for the discussion of principles, but also laboratories for definite investigation. In a few generations many natural sciences and human studies were established in these schools. We may assume that even before Plato some order and constancy in training and common work had united not only the Pythagoreans but also the pupils of other earlier thinkers with their masters and one another. In the bright light of attested history the Academy and the Peripatetic School then confront us as legal organizations, in which the unity of basic philosophical thought held the particular sciences together, and the passion for pure knowledge of the truth imparted to every definite work a life and relation to the whole—an unrivalled example of the creative power of such an organization. Plato's school was long a center of mathematical and astronomic enquiry. But the group around Aristotle completed the greatest scientific task ever performed in one place and in so brief a time. The basic ideas of teleological structure and development, the method of description, analysis, and comparison, led in this school to the establishment of the descriptive and analytic natural sciences, of politics and aesthetics.

In this organization of philosophical schools the Greek concept of philosophy as the all-inclusive science found its fullest expression—an example of an essential aspect of philosophy: a common task combines the philosophizing persons in a common activity. For wherever many persons share a purpose, it interconnects them. So in philosophy a unifying power lies in its tendency to universality and universal validity.

The unitary control of scientific work, which found its highest development in the school of Aristotle, fell apart like the empire of Alexander. The particular sciences then grew independent as they matured. The bond which had held them together broke. Outside of the philosophical schools the followers of Alexander established institutions which served the interests of these sciences. Here was a first factor, changing the status of philosophy. The particular sciences gradually took over the whole realm of existent reality in a movement which began again in the modern period and has not ended even yet. Whenever philosophy had led some field of enquiry almost to maturity, the protégé cut the leading strings. Such was the case at first with the natural sciences; then in modern times this differentiation increased. Since Hugo Grotius general jurisprudence has become independent, and since Montesquieu comparative theory of the state. Today the struggle for the emancipation of their science is winning the respect of psychologists, and as the general sciences of religion, art, teaching, and society are based on the study of historical facts and on psychology, their relation to philosophy must also be questioned. From outside of philosophy, as it were, this ever increasing disarrangement of the composition of forces within the sphere of knowledge set the task of marking off philosophical boundaries anew. In its inner development, however, lay far stronger causes of this.

The coöperation of that outer factor and the forces working from within now brought about a change of philosophical attitude, a change growing from the advent of the Sceptics, Epicureans, and Stoics to the writings of Cicero, Lucretius, Seneca, Epictetus, and Marcus Aurelius. Within the new composition of forces in the field of knowledge the failure of metaphysics, the diffusion of the sceptical spirit, and the turning of the aging nations to inwardness all made themselves felt. The philosophy of life developed. In it we meet a new attitude of the philosophical spirit, which was to be permanently of the greatest significance. The problem of the great systems was still held fast in its whole scope. Yet the claim to its universally valid solution was taken more and more indulgently. The hierarchy of individual problems changed; the cosmological problem was subordinated to the problem of the value and purpose of life. In the Roman-Stoic system, the most influential which the world has seen, the character-building power of philosophy came to the fore. There was a change of philosophical structure, the order and relation of parts. The appearance of new definitions of philosophy corresponded to this shift of philosophical attitude. Cicero sees in philosophy "the teacher of life, the discoverer of laws, the guide to every virtue," and Seneca defines it as the theory and art of the correct conduct of life. In other words, philosophy is a way of life, not mere theory, and so the expression 'wisdom' is readily applied to it. But if one returns from the new concept of philosophy to the attitude which it expresses, philosophy is seen to have developed nevertheless in perfect continuity out of the great metaphysical systems. Its problem was merely subjected to new conditions.

For long centuries, as this undertow into the unfathomable depths of the essence of things then led the aging world to religion, philosophy in its subordination to religion was not itself. The philosophical attitude at this time toward the problem of universal and universally valid knowledge, the concepts of philosophy which thus arose, are not strictly relevant to the unfolding of its essence. They will be considered in the theory of the connecting links between philosophy and religion.

2. *The Forms of Modern Philosophy as they have been Expressed in the Definitions of Philosophy*

After the preparations of the Renaissance, where a secularized art, literature, and free, literary philosophy of life were culturally dominant, the sciences of nature were finally being established and the sciences of society were becoming for the first time in the empirical order a coherent group, derived from one idea. Thus the sciences of experience were trying to know the universe by their methods. In this context a new pattern of cultural forces arose in the seventeenth century. Zeal for strict, universally valid knowledge and for its application to transform the world pervaded the leading nations. As this knowledge united the particular sciences and philosophy, they thus became most sharply opposed to the religious attitude, and left art, literature, and philosophy of life behind them. Hence the trend toward universally valid cosmological knowledge, such as had prevailed in the great systems of antiquity, continued even more persistently and methodically under the new conditions. So also the character and the concept of metaphysics were altered. It had progressed from a naïve attitude toward the world, through doubt, to a clear understanding of the relation of thought to this world. Now metaphysics, aware of its peculiar method, drew away from the particular sciences. Now also it found its proper object in the being which is given to us in no particular science as such. But distinctive features of the new metaphysical development were the methodological demand for strict, universal validity and the growing reflection on metaphysical method. That demand united metaphysics with the mathematical natural sciences, and the methodological nature of universality and of proof from first principles separated it from them. So it was time to establish the method adequate to this new consciousness of method.

a) *The New Concept of Metaphysics.* Immediately after establishing mechanics Descartes undertook to use his new constructive method to determine the nature of philosophy. The first characteristic of this method, in contrast with that of the particular sciences, lay in the very general view of the problem and in the regress from the first assumptions in this view to a highest principle. Here the method merely brought features, implicit in the nature of philosophy, to a fuller expression than any earlier system. But its unique brilliance lay in the manner of execution. The mathematical natural sciences contain presuppositions which lie beyond the particular fields of mathematics, mechanics, and astronomy. If one presents these presuppositions in clear concepts and propositions, and understands why they are objectively valid, a constructive method can be built on them. In this way the mechanistic view first won its certainty and showed the possibility of further extension. Descartes urged this against Galileo, and herein he saw the superiority of the philosopher to the physicist. Then Hobbes and Spinoza used the same constructive method. Spinoza's new pantheistic system of the identity of mind and nature arose precisely in the application of this method to reality—whose given properties, of course, he always presupposed. His system was an interpretation of empirical reality on the basis of simple, self-evident truths. From this metaphysics of identity came the doctrine of the causal nexus of mental states, which leads through the bondage, imposed by the passions, to freedom. Finally, Leibniz carried the method further than anyone else. Till his death he was occupied with the Herculean task of elaborating his new universal logic as a basis of constructive procedure. The use of method as a criterion of philosophy has survived in metaphysical systems since the seventeenth century.

The constructive method of these thinkers then succumbed to the critique of knowledge by Locke, Hume, and Kant, even though in Leibniz epistemological foundations survived, which have only very recently been fully appreciated. The thesis, that the clarity and distinctness of simple concepts and the self-evidence of simple propositions proves their objective validity, turned out to be untenable. The categories of substance, causality, and purpose were reduced to indispensable conditions for cognitive consciousness. Although the certainty of mathematics had guaranteed this constructive philosophical method, yet Kant showed in intuition the distinctive basis of mathematical evidence. And also the constructive method in the human studies, as seen in law and natural theology, proved unable to do justice to the fullness of the historical world in thought and political action. Accordingly, drastic reform of metaphysical procedure was necessary to avoid the repudiation of every characteristically metaphysical method. And Kant himself, who overthrew the constructive method of philosophy, showed the way to such a transformation. In the method which he called transcendental he saw the distinctive aspect of his critical life-work and, such a critique being for him the chief concern of philosophy, the distinctive aspect of philosophy itself. The edifice which he planned to erect in this way was to be based on the truths thus discovered, and in this sense he retained the term 'metaphysics.' He had already grasped even the new principle of content on which Schelling, Schleiermacher, Hegel, Schopenhauer, Fechner, and Lotze established metaphysics.

According to the great insight of the new epistemological philosophy of Locke, Hume, and Kant, the external world is only a phenomenon. Reality is given in the facts of consciousness (for the English thinkers, directly; for Kant, to be sure, conceptually, subject to the conditions of consciousness). But this reality—that is the decisive novelty in Kant's standpoint—is the systematic unity of mind, and every systematic unity in external reality is reducible to it. Accordingly, the simple concepts and propositions, which the constructive philosophy had made basic, are only elements of this unity, isolated by the understanding and abstractly formulated. From Kant's conception the new German metaphysics set out. Hence the German metaphysicians from Schelling to Schopenhauer looked with hate and contempt at "reflection" and "understanding," which deal with substances, causal relations, and purposes—these abstract elements of a living thing. With their new method, proceeding from the systematic unity of mind, they could at last do justice to the human studies, which had grown superficial and trivial through the application of those concepts of reflection. And this very assumption of mental unity carried the concept of evolution, empirically confirmed in nature, over into the fruitful idea of development. It was the last and most complete attempt to develop an appropriate philosophical method. A gigantic endeavor! But even so it had to fail. In consciousness, it is true, lies the possibility of grasping the order of the world. And at least the formal operations, through which consciousness does this, are necessary. But even this metaphysical method does not find the bridge, leading from necessity as a fact of our consciousness to objective validity. And in vain it seeks a way from the systematic unity of consciousness to the insight that this unity is the inner bond of reality itself.

So the possibilities of metaphysical method were now tried

out in Germany, one after the other, and always with the same negative result. During the nineteenth century two of them contended for dominance. Schelling, Schleiermacher, Hegel, and Schopenhauer advanced from the systematic unity of consciousness, and each of them thus discovered his principle of the universe. With Herbart as a foundation, Lotze and Fechner started out from what is given in consciousness as a sum-total of experiences, and tried to prove that a consistent conceptual knowledge of what is here given is possible only through the reduction of the given sensory world to mental facts and connections. The first group advanced from Kant and Fichte, who had aimed to raise philosophy to a universally valid science. The second group reached back primarily to Leibniz, for whom the explanation of the world had been only a well-founded hypothesis. The ablest thinkers in the first movement, Schelling and Hegel, started with Fichte's proposition that the universally valid, systematic unity of consciousness, manifesting itself in the empirical ego, produces the systematic unity of the universe. This proposition itself was a false interpretation of the facts of consciousness. But now, by believing themselves entitled to change the systematic unity which they assumed in consciousness, since this unity preconditions the world appearing in consciousness, into the systematic unity of the universe itself, the pure ego into the world-ground, they transcended the bounds of possible experience. In restless dialectic, from the intellectual intuition of Fichte and Schelling to the dialectical method of Hegel, they vainly sought a procedure to prove the identity of logical coherence and the nature of things, of the systematic unity in consciousness and that in the universe. The contradiction between the cosmos which they thus found and the order of phenomenal laws, established by the empirical sciences, utterly annihilated their position. But the other movement, based on Herbart, led by Lotze and Fechner, and resolved to gain consistent conceptual knowledge of the given by the hypothesis of a spiritual unity, fell foul of an inner dialectic no less disruptive. The way from the manifold of empirical data to the sources of all things through concepts, unverifiable by any observation, led them into a night in which "reals" or "monads," the temporal or the timeless, a universal Consciousness equivalent to an Unconscious, might be found by explanatory profundity. They heaped up hypotheses, which in the inaccessible realm beyond experience found no firm ground, but also no resistance. Here one set of hypotheses was just as plausible as another. How could this metaphysics have fulfilled the mission of giving certainty and security to individual and social life in the great crises of the century!

And so even this last and most ambitious attempt of the human mind failed to find a philosophical method, distinct from the procedure of the empirical sciences, on which a metaphysics could be based. The world given in experience, knowledge of which is the work of the particular sciences, cannot be made more deeply intelligible by a metaphysical method distinct from theirs.

b) *The New Non-metaphysical Definitions of Philosophy.* Thought is driven on to other possibilities by the inner dialectic of the problem: to secure a concept of the nature of philosophy as significant in its own right, independently of the particular sciences. If no method can be found to guarantee the title of metaphysics to existence beside the empirical sciences, then philosophy must satisfy in new ways the need of the mind for universality, for grounding in principle, and for grasp of reality. The standpoint of scepticism must be overcome even in the new field of investigation. Groping forward, philosophy seeks an attitude of consciousness toward the given which would do justice to the situation created by the newly established empirical sciences. And if a method cannot be found which provides for philosophy its own object, a being like substance, God, or soul, from which the results of the particular sciences would be deducible, then thought considers next the possibility of proceeding from the objective knowledge of the particular sciences themselves and seeking to ground it in the theory of knowledge.

For one field is indisputably proper to philosophy. If the particular sciences have divided among themselves the realm of given reality, and each deals with a section of it, yet precisely in this way a new realm arises, these sciences themselves. We turn our attention from the real to the knowledge of it, and find here a field which lies beyond the particular sciences. Ever since human reflection discovered this field, it has been constantly recognized as the domain of philosophy—theory of theories, logic, epistemology. If one takes the field in its full extent, then philosophy includes the whole theory of the logical grounding of the knowledge involved in the recognition of facts, the determination of values, the establishment of goals, and the imposition of laws. And if now the whole concept of knowledge, as such is its object, then philosophy includes the mutual relations of the particular sciences, their necessary order, each new science presupposing the earlier ones and raising itself upon them with the facts belonging to its own field. With this epistemological point of view the spirit of foundation and of coherence grows even in the particular sciences themselves. The social impulse of these sciences in universities and academies fosters the spirit, and the important task of philosophy in these institutions is to keep it alive. The classical representative of this epistemological standpoint within the empirical sciences themselves is Helmholtz. He has based the right of philosophy to a place beside the particular sciences on the fact that it has in knowledge its distinctive object. The necessary business "of examining the sources of our knowledge and the degree of its justification" will always be left for philosophy, which "has its great significance in the circle of the sciences as the theory of the sources and activities of knowledge, in the sense of Kant and (so far as I have understood him) the elder Fichte."

While the essential activity of philosophy was transferred to epistemology, nevertheless the relation of philosophy to its basic problem was preserved. Epistemology had developed precisely in the critique of the aim to know objectively the world-order and world-ground, supreme value and ultimate goal. Out of this fruitless metaphysical labor sprang the inquiry concerning the bounds of human knowledge. And epistemology in the course of its development came gradually to comprehend the most universal position of consciousness in relation to its data, a position which therefore also expresses most fully our relation to the riddle of the world and of life. It is the position which Plato had already admitted: philosophy is the reflection of the mind on all of its general attitudes and their ultimate presuppositions. Kant has assigned to philosophy the same position as Plato. The breadth of his view is shown in the equal extension of his critical and constructive epistemology to knowledge of facts, to the judgment of aesthetic values, to the examination of the teleological principle in the interpretation of nature, and to the universally valid deduction of moral laws. And as every philosophical standpoint involves the attempt to advance from the comprehension of reality to establish rules of conduct, so also this epistemological standpoint has always developed in its greatest advocates the tendency to stress the practical, reformative influence of philosophy and its character-building power. Indeed, Kant declares that the concept of philosophy as aiming at the logical completeness of knowledge is only an academic notion. "But," he adds, "there is also a lay notion of philosophy as the science of the relation of all knowledge to the essential aims of human reason." Our concern is now, in Kant's language, to find the connection between the academic and the lay notion. The present neo-Kantian school has met this demand in distinguished works.

A different non-metaphysical position arose in the circle of the individual investigators themselves. It is content with the conceptual description of the phenomenal world and with the proof of its lawful order by experimental trial and the appearance of theoretically precalculated effects. If epistemology proceeds from the positive nature of the results of the particular sciences, if it can add to these sciences no new items of objective knowledge, and can find no new proofs from principle within the system of theirs, then the possibility remains of adhering once for all to the positive character of the results of these sciences, of finding the fixed point, which the new philosophizing seeks, in their practically proved self-sufficiency for the comprehension of the given, and of renouncing as fruitless every reflection concerning their universal validity. And if one follows the long chains of epistemological reasoning, the difficulties of forming concepts in this field, and the strife of factions, these are weighty motives for choosing this new philosophical position. So philosophy shifts its center to the consciousness of the logical system of the sciences, and in this new position seems finally to reach an objective view of the world, free from metaphysical and epistemological investigations. If the empirical sciences explore the particular divisions or aspects of reality, then they leave for philosophy the task of understanding the inner relations of these sciences to one another, through which together they enable us to know the whole of reality.

Philosophy, then, is an encyclopedia of the sciences in a higher, philosophical sense. In the later part of antiquity, after the particular sciences had become independent, encyclopedias appeared. Academic activity demanded them, and an inventory of the great works of the ancient world was needed. Moreover—

what is important for us here—after the Nordic incursion and, following the West Roman Empire, the first establishment of the Germanic and Romanic states on the soil of the ancient culture with its implements, from Martianus Capella on, such encyclopedic works (even though still crudely) preserved ancient thought concerning the description of the world in the sciences. In the three great works of Vincent of Beauvais such a concept of the encyclopedia was most perfectly represented. From this cataloguing of knowledge, which went on through the Middle Ages, the modern philosophical encyclopedia now issued. Its basic work stemmed from Chancellor Bacon. Starting with him, the encyclopedia consciously sought the principle of the necessary relations of the sciences. Hobbes first discovered this principle in their natural order of logical dependence in a linear series. Then in connection with the French *Encyclopedia* d'Alembert and Turgot methodically applied the concept of philosophy as the universal science. And on this basis Comte finally presented positive philosophy as the system of the essential relations of logical and historical dependence among the sciences, together with their termination in sociology. From this standpoint a methodological analysis of the particular sciences was made. The structure of each was examined, their presuppositions were established, and in these the principle of the interrelations of the sciences was obtained. It could also be shown how in this progress from science to science new methods arose. Finally, in this way, sociology was demanded and methodologically planned as the proper business of philosophy. And that fulfilled the tendency, planted in the positive sciences with their separation from the parent stem, to derive their systematic interconnection from themselves without additional reference to a general epistemological basis, hence as positive philosophy. It was a significant attempt, to make philosophy the immanent system of objective knowledge. This positivistic view of philosophy proceeds from the rigorous concept of universally valid knowledge, a concept developed in the mathematical natural sciences. Accordingly, the broader significance of the view for philosophical activity lies in the fact that it vindicates the claims thus arising and purifies the sciences of every undemonstrable corollary, derived from metaphysical conceptions. To be sure, through this essential opposition to metaphysics the new position is conditioned historically by metaphysics. More broadly, however, what connects this branch of philosophy also with its trunk is the tendency to a universal and universally valid understanding of the world.

But this second non-metaphysical position now extends far beyond the field of positivism. Through the subordination of mental facts to the knowledge of nature a *Weltanschauung* is mingled with positivism, which thus becomes a particular doctrine within the new position. We find the same position widely adopted also without this supplement, and, indeed, by many distinguished scholars in the field of the human studies. In political science and jurisprudence it appears in a singularly effective way. The view of the imperatives which legislation imposes upon the citizens of a state can be restricted to the interpretation of the will expressed in these imperatives, and to logical analysis and historical explanation, without a return to universal principles, like, for example, the idea of justice, to support and validate positive law. Such a procedure implies a philosophical position akin to positivism.

Especially in contemporary France this positivistic view of reality finds its power limited—great though it is today even there—in the inability of its phenomenal mode of interpretation to do justice to the reality of the historical consciousness and of the collective values of life. And for that very reason this position, as a positive interpretation of legal systems, is in no position to establish ideals which could guide an age headed for the transformation of society.

The epistemological movement sought the distinctive feature of philosophy in its methodological attitude, and reflection on its own method, namely, the search of philosophy for ultimate presuppositions, made progress in this movement. On the other hand, positive thought sought the characteristic feature of philosophy in its function within the system of the sciences, and the striving of philosophy for universality advanced in this thought. But there still remained the possibility of so seeking the peculiar object of philosophy as to satisfy its aspiration to grasp reality. Despite the failure of the attempts to force the gates of reality on the metaphysical road, the reality of consciousness as a fact stood out all the more sharply in its significance. In inner experience we are given this reality of consciousness, and with it the possibility of knowing more profoundly from their source the various products of the human mind as they are understood in the human studies. Inner experience is the starting point for logic, epistemology, and every theory of the production of a unitary world-view, and the basis for psychology, aesthetics, ethics, and related disciplines. The whole field thus circumscribed has always been called philosophical. This situation accounts for that view of the nature of philosophy which conceives it as science of inner experience or as science of mind.

This standpoint was developed after the elaboration of the theory of association gave to eighteenth century psychology an empirical basis, and a broad realm of fruitful applications in epistemology, aesthetics, and ethics opened before it. David Hume in his *Treatise of Human Nature* saw in the empirical study of man the true philosophy. As he repudiated metaphysics, based epistemology exclusively on the new psychology, and in this psychology also showed the explanatory principles for the human studies, an introspectively grounded system of these studies arose. After the formation of the natural sciences this system, centered in the theory of man, contained the other and greater task for the human mind. Adam Smith, Bentham, James Mill, John Stuart Mill, and Bain labored on at it. John Stuart Mill, like Hume, wanted philosophy to mean "the scientific knowledge of man as an intellectual, moral, and social being." In Germany Beneke represented the same standpoint. He took it over from the English and Scottish school, and only in its elaboration was he influenced by Herbart. In this sense he had declared already in his *Foundation for the Physics of Morals*: "If my view prevails, the whole of philosophy becomes the natural science of the human mind." He was guided by the great truth that inner experience discloses to us a complete reality in the inner life, while the outer world is given to us in the senses as mere appearance. And he then showed in his *Pragmatic Psychology* how "all that confronts us as subject-matter to be known in logic, morality, aesthetics, philosophy of religion, and, indeed, even in metaphysics" can be clearly and deeply comprehended only "when we view it according to the basic laws of mental development in man, as (theoretical) psychology presents them in their most general interconnections." Among the later thinkers Theodor Lipps in his *Basic Facts of the Inner Life* has expressly defined philosophy as the science of mind or science of inner experience.

The great contribution of these thinkers to the development

of the human studies is beyond doubt. Only since the basic position of psychology in this field has been recognized and our items of psychological knowledge have been applied to the particular human studies, have these begun to approximate the demands of universally valid knowledge. But philosophy in its new position as science of inner experience could not answer the question as to the universal validity of scientific knowledge. And in its restricted scope it could not do justice even to the task which positivism rightly set for itself. Thus Theodor Lipps also has advanced to a new understanding of his position.

This view of philosophy clearly reveals a supremely significant relation of the third non-metaphysical position to the metaphysical problems, a relation confirmed by the use of terms and the course of history. Natural sciences lift out of lived experience only partial contents which can help to determine changes in the physical world, independent of us. So knowledge of nature deals merely with appearances for consciousness. The subject-matter of the human studies, on the other hand, is the inwardly given reality of the lived experiences themselves. Here, therefore, we possess a reality, lived—to be sure, only lived—which philosophy longs incessantly to comprehend. One sees how even this outline of a definition of philosophy preserves an essential continuity with its original, basic problem.

3. *Conclusion concerning the Essence of Philosophy*

In one sense the result of our historical survey is negative. In each of the definitions of philosophy only one aspect of its essence appears. Each of them is merely the expression of a standpoint which philosophy adopted at one stage in its history. Each states what to one or more thinkers in a certain context seemed requisite and possible as its rôle. Each of them defines a particular group of phenomena as philosophy, excluding from this group the other things often so called. The great oppositions of standpoints, contending with equal force, gain expression in the definitions. They assert themselves over against one another with equal justification. And the dispute can be settled only if a standpoint above the factions can be found.

So the point of view for formulating each of the previous definitions is that of the systematic philosopher who seeks from the context of his system to express in a definition what seems to him a worthy and feasible task for philosophy. In this he is certainly justified, but then he is defining his own philosophy. He does not deny that philosophy in the course of history has set itself other tasks also, but he declares their accomplishment impossible or worthless, and so the labor involved seems to him a long-lingering illusion. As far as the individual philosopher is clearly aware of this meaning of his definition, he is undoubtedly justified in restricting philosophy to epistemology, to the sciences growing out of inner experience, or to the systematic order of all the sciences, in which they achieve knowledge.

The problem of so defining philosophy as to explain the use of the term and the views of individual philosophers concerning the subject leads necessarily from the systematic to the historical standpoint. We must determine, not what now or here passes as philosophy, but what always and everywhere constitutes its essence. All the particular concepts of philosophy only point to this universal essence, which explains its various appearances and the differences among these views. The superiority of this historical standpoint is proved by the very fact that it enables us to understand as necessary the self-certainty with which the particular systems appear in their uniqueness and express themselves concerning philosophy. When viewed historically, every solution of a philosophical problem belongs to a situation present at that time. Man, this temporal creature, maintains the security of his existence, as long as he works in time, by lifting his creations out of the temporal flux as enduring objects. While under this illusion he creates with greater joy and power. Herein lies the eternal contradiction between the creative and the historical consciousness. The former naturally tries to forget the past and to ignore the better in the future. But the latter lives in the synthesis of all times, and it perceives in all individual creation the accompanying relativity and transience. This contradiction is the silently born affliction most characteristic of philosophy today. For in the contemporary philosopher his own creative activity is co-present with the historical consciousness, since at present his philosophy without this would embrace only a fragment of reality. He must recognize his creative activity as a part of the historical continuum, in which he consciously produces something dependent. Then a resolution of this contradiction becomes possible for him, as will later appear. Now he can calmly submit to the authority of the historical consciousness, and he can view even his own daily work from the historical system, in which the essence of philosophy is realized in the variety of its appearances.

In this historical view every particular concept of philosophy becomes an instance, referring to the formative law which the essence of philosophy contains. And however untenable in itself each of the definitions may be, when formulated from the systematic standpoint, yet now they are all important for answering the question as to the essence of philosophy. Indeed, they are an essential part of the historical facts from which we are now to reason.

For this conclusion we gather up all the empirical data of our survey. We found the term 'philosophy' assigned to situations of very different kinds. We saw that philosophy is extraordinarily mobile, always setting itself new tasks and adjusting itself to the conditions of culture. It takes up problems as worth while and then discards them. At one stage of knowledge it regards questions as answerable, and then drops them later on as unanswerable. But we always saw working in it the same tendency toward universality and logical grounding, the same direction of the mind toward the whole of the given world. And the metaphysical urge to penetrate into the heart of this whole constantly struggles with the positivistic demand of philosophy for universally valid knowledge. Those are the two sides of its essence which distinguish it from even the most closely related fields of culture. Unlike the particular sciences philosophy seeks to solve the very riddle of the world and of life; unlike art and religion it tries to present this solution in universally valid form. For that is the chief result emerging from the historical evidence discussed: an insulated logical and historical continuum leads from the metaphysics of the Greeks, who undertook to solve the great riddle of the world and of life with universal validity, to the most radical positivists or sceptics of the present. The fortunes of philosophy are all determined somehow by this starting point and the basic philosophical problem. All possible attitudes of the human mind to the riddle are surveyed. In this historical continuum the contribution of each particular position of philosophy is the realization of one possibility under the given conditions. Each expresses an essential feature of philosophy, while its limitations point to the teleological system on which it depends as part of a whole, which alone contains the whole truth. This complex of historical facts is explained by the rôle of philosophy as a function in the purposive system of society, which is determined by the peculiar contribution of philosophy. How philosophy performs this function in its particular positions depends on its relation to the whole and also on the cultural situation in respect to time, place, circumstances of life, and personality. Hence philosophy tolerates no fixed boundaries imposed by a definite material or method.

This state of affairs, which forms the essence of philosophy, binds together all philosophical thinkers. Here we find the explanation of an essential feature which has confronted us in the appearances of philosophy. As we saw, this term signifies something uniformly recurrent, which is present wherever the term occurs; but it signifies at the same time a necessary connection of the participants. If philosophy is a definite function in society, then it intimately relates those in whom this purpose lives. The leaders of philosophical schools are thus united with their pupils. In the academies which gained prominence after the establishment of the particular sciences we found these sciences in coöperation, supplementing one another and sustained by the idea of the unity of knowledge, an idea present in philosophers like Plato, Aristotle, and Leibniz. Finally, during the eighteenth century the universities also grew into organizations for scientific collaboration, uniting teachers with one another and with pupils, and here also philosophy had the function of keeping alive the consciousness of the grounding, the unity, and the goal of knowledge. All these organizations are included in the inner purposive system in which, from Thales and Pythagoras on, one thinker propounds problems and transmits truths to another. Possibilities of solution are thought through in such a sequence; the formation of *Weltanschauungen* continues. The great thinkers influence every subsequent age.

III. THE CONNECTING LINKS BETWEEN PHILOSOPHY AND RELIGION, PROSE, AND POETRY

The systems of the great thinkers, in which philosophy is presented *par excellence,* and the historical continuity of these systems have led us to a pregnant insight into the function of philosophy. But still the application of 'philosophy' and 'philosophical' cannot be fully derived from this function. These terms are extended also to manifestations which it does not determine exclusively. Our horizon must be enlarged to explain these facts.

The kinship of philosophy with religion, prose, and poetry has been continually noted. An essential relation to the riddle of the world and of life is common to all three. And thus 'philosophy' and 'philosophical,' or cognate terms, have been transferred to products of the religious attitude, of the experience and conduct of life, of literary activity in prose and poetry.

The Greek apologists call Christianity simply philosophy. According to Justin, Christ, as the divine reason become man, definitely settles the question with which the true philosophers have wrestled. And for Minucius Felix, philosophy, which is completed in Christianity, consists in the eternal truths about God, human responsibility, and immortality, which are grounded in reason and are rationally demonstrable. The Christians, he said, are today the (true) philosophers, and the philosophers in pagan times were already Christians. Another very important Christian group uses *gnosis* for the knowledge which completes faith. The heretical *gnosis* has its roots in the experience of Christianity's moral power to free the soul from sensuality, and this group interprets the experience metaphysically in the case of intuitions appearing in religious history. Within the Church Clement of Alexandria conceived *gnosis* as Christian faith, raised to knowledge, and ascribed to it the right to expound the higher meaning of the Holy Scriptures. In his treatise, *On the Principles*, the complete system of the ecclesiastical *gnosis*, Origen defines this as the procedure which establishes on a rational basis the truths contained in the tradition of the Apostles. And within the contemporary Graeco-Roman speculation an analogous connecting link appears in Neo-Platonism. For here the philosophical impulse finds its ultimate satisfaction in mystical union with the Godhead, thus in a religious event. Hence Porphyry sees the theme and goal of philosophy in the salvation of the soul, and Proclus prefers 'theology' to 'philosophy' as the term for his mode of thought. The conceptual means for inwardly unifying religion and philosophy are the same in all these systems. The first is the doctrine of *logos*. In the divine unity is a power to communicate itself, and so the philosophical and religious forms of communication proceed from God in essential relation. The other means is allegorical interpretation, through which the particular and historical element in religious belief and the Holy Scriptures is raised to a universal *Weltanschauung*. In the systems themselves philosophical impulse, religious faith, rational proof, and mystical union with the Godhead are so bound up together that the religious and the philosophical processes are presented as aspects of the same process. For in this age of great religious struggle the observation of the development of significant personalities suggests the new creative thought that there is a general type for the genetic history of the more exalted souls. On this thought the highest forms of medieval mysticism are based, so that in them also one may recognize not a mere mixture of these two fields but, for deep psychological insight, their essential unity. The necessary consequence of such a spiritual phenomenon was a complete terminological upheaval. Jakob Boehme calls his life-work a holy philosophy.

Although all these facts point to the inner relation of religion and philosophy, yet it is finally revealed in the inability of the history of philosophy to exclude these connecting links from itself. They have their place in the progress from experience of life to psychological awareness of this experience, as in the origin and development of a view of life. Thus this intermediate zone between religion and philosophy makes it necessary to go back behind the essential features of philosophy, until now firmly established, to contexts of broader scope and deeper foundation.

The same necessity results also, when we look at the relations of philosophy to experience of life and to the literature of prose and poetry as these relations are shown in terminology, definition, and historical connection. Authors, striving to gain a secure standpoint for their influence on the public, find themselves on this road with those who are proceeding from philosophical investigation itself and, in despair of system, are aiming to establish and express the knowledge of life more freely and humanely.

Lessing can be regarded as representative of the first class. By nature he was a writer. Although as a young man he was aware of the philosophical systems, he did not think of taking part in the strife. But each of the tasks, great and small, which he set himself compelled him to seek fixed concepts and truths. Whoever intends to lead the public must himself be on a sure road. So he was led on from restricted problems to ever more general ones. Without going through the systematic work of the philosophers he solved these problems with the power of his own nature, as time had formed it. Out of life itself an ideal of life arose in him. From the philosophy around him he received the deterministic doctrine, and it was confirmed by the men he knew so well. Then, on these foundations his theological studies provided a certain idea of the divine power in which the necessary connection of things is grounded. These and other related elements led him thus, in a sense, to an inner structure of his ideas, but this structure is still very different from the essential features of philosophy as they have been presented. And yet no one hesitates to speak of Lessing's philosophy. At a definite point he lays hold of the history of this region of life and there asserts his place. Accordingly, in all the authors of whom he is typical we are dealing with an intermediate zone, which joins philosophy and literature.

The very same zone contains also the other group, which proceeded from systematic philosophy to a more subjective, formless kind to solve the riddle of life and the world. In the history of the human mind this group occupies a very prominent place. Especially, whenever an era of systematic thinking has ended, whenever its prevalent values of life no longer fit the altered human situation, and its conceptual knowledge of the world, finely and subtly elaborated, can no longer take account of newly experienced facts, such thinkers come forward and proclaim a new day in the life of philosophy. Examples of this are those philosophers of the Stoic-Roman school who, starting in moral philosophy, came to discard the burden of Greek system and to seek their goal in a freer interpretation of life itself. Marcus Aurelius, whose monologues are the most inspired form for this procedure, sees the essence of philosophy in a quality of life which preserves the God within us free from the world's power and unspotted by its dirt. Yet in the system of the Stoic doctrine these thinkers had a solid background for their view of life, and so they were still intimately connected with the movement of the philosophy which is subject to the requirement of universal validity. Indeed, in this philosophy they have their place as a further development of the doctrine of personality erected on pantheistic determinism. This trend has returned in nineteenth-century German philosophy, and here also, because of the character of such a doctrine, it shows a strong tendency to freer expressions. But even more clearly a series of modern thinkers has diverged from philosophy with its demand for universal validity. The art of experiencing and conducting life in the Renaissance perfected the essays of Montaigne as its finest flower. He leaves behind him the judgment of life in medieval philosophy, and even more decisively than Marcus Aurelius surrenders every claim to proof from principles and to universal validity. Only in occasional and brief writings do his works extend beyond the study of man: for him his essays are his philosophy. For philosophy is the sculptress of judgment and morals; indeed, at bottom constancy and uprightness are the true philosophy. And as Montaigne himself calls his work philosophy, in his place he is indispensable in the history of this sphere of life. In the same way, Carlyle, Emerson, Ruskin, Nietzsche, even Tolstoy and Maeterlinck in the present, have some relation to systematic philosophy, and yet still more consciously, more firmly than Montaigne they turn away from it, still more consistently they have broken every bond with philosophy as a science.

Like mysticism, these phenomena are no cloudy mixture of philosophy and another field, but symptoms of a mental development. Let us seek to grasp the essence of this modern philosophy of life. It forms one side of philosophy, as the methodological requirements of universal validity and logical grounding are gradually relaxed. The explanation of life from experience of life gradually achieves freer and freer forms. Insights are united in unsystematic but impressive interpretations. In its substitution of persuasion for orderly proof this kind of writing is akin to the ancient art of the sophists and rhetoricians, whom Plato banished so sternly from the realm of philosophy. And yet a strong, inner relation joins some of these thinkers with the philosophical movement itself. Their art of persuasion is strangely combined with an awful seriousness and a great sincerity. Their eyes remain focused on the riddle of life, but they despair of solving it by a universally valid metaphysics, a theory of the world-order. Life is to be explained in terms of itself— that is the great thought that links these writers with experience of the world and with poetry. From Schopenhauer on, this thought has been developed with ever greater hostility to systematic philosophy. Now it forms the center of philosophical interest for the younger generation. A literary trend of peculiar magnitude and independence is revealed in these writings. And, since their authors claim to be philosophers, they are preparing the way today, as the religious thinkers once did, for new developments of systematic philosophy. For, after the "universally valid science" of metaphysics is forever destroyed, a method independent of it must be found to determine values, goals, and rules of life. And on the basis of the descriptive and analytic psychology which proceeds from the structure of the inner life we shall have to seek within systematic knowledge for a solution, even if a more modest and less dogmatic solution, of this problem, which the contemporary philosophers of life have set themselves.

The complex relation between religion, philosophy, experience of life, and poetry, which appears in this zone, necessitates our return to the relations of the cultural forces in the individual person and in society. As the uncertainty concerning limits is grounded in the fluidity of philosophical criteria and refers to the definition of philosophy as a function, this uncertainty can be wholly understood only when we return to the system of life in the individual and in society, and introduce philosophy into it. That involves the application of a new method.

Second Part

THE ESSENCE OF PHILOSOPHY UNDERSTOOD FROM ITS POSITION IN THE WORLD OF MIND

Thus far the essential features of philosophy have been inductively derived from the instances called philosophy and from the concepts formed of them in the history of philosophy. These features referred us to a function of philosophy as a general attitude in society. And through this general attitude we found all philosophizing persons united in the inner continuity of the history of philosophy. Then in various intermediate forms philosophy appeared in the regions of religion, reflection on life, and the literature of prose and poetry. These inductions from the historical facts are now to be confirmed and combined in the definitive knowledge of the essence of philosophy, by placing philosophy in the system in which it performs its function. So its concept is to be completed by showing its relation to the concepts above it and those coördinate with it.

I. Placement of the Functions of Philosophy in the System of Mental Life, of Society, and of History

1. *The Position of Philosophy in the Structure of Mental Life*

We understand historically given facts only from the inwardness of mental life. The science which describes and analyzes this inwardness is descriptive psychology. Hence it comprehends also—as it were, from within—the function of philosophy in the economy of mental life, and determines the function in relation to its next of kin among the mental activities. So this psychology completes the concept of the essence of philosophy. For the concepts under which that of philosophy belongs concern the inner relations of characteristics which are integrated through lived experience and understanding of other persons into a real system. Theoretical natural science, on the other hand, merely ascertains uniformities in sensory phenomena.

All human creations spring from the inner life and its relations to the outer world. As science always seeks **regularities**, the study of mental creations must start out from **the regulari-**

ties in mental life. These are of two kinds. The inner life shows uniformities which can be established through its changes. These uniformities we treat as we treat external nature. Science ascertains them by separating particular processes from the complex lived experiences and inductively disclosing uniformities in these processes. Thus we come to know the processes of association, reproduction, or apperception. Every change is here a case of the uniformities. They constitute one aspect of the psychological basis for explaining mental creations. Thus the peculiar formative processes in which perceptions are transformed into pictures of fantasy contain a partial explanation of myth, saga, legend, and artistic creation. But the events of the inner life are joined by relations of another kind. As parts they are united in the system of mental life. This system I call the mental structure. It is the pattern in which diverse mental facts are united in mature mental life by a relation which can be lived. The basic form of this inner system is determined by the reciprocity in which all mental life is conditioned by its environment and reacts purposively to it. Sensations are evoked and represent the variety of their outer causes. Stimulated by the relation of those causes to our own life, as the relation is expressed in feeling, we attend to these impressions, we apperceive, distinguish, unite, judge, and reason. Under the influence of objective awareness the basic manifold of feeling gives rise to more and more correct evaluations of life's aspects and of the external causes of this inner life and the system of its impulses. Guided by these evaluations, we alter the character of the environment through appropriate conduct, or through inner volition we adjust our own conscious processes to our needs. That is human life. And in its system perception, memory, thought, impulse, feeling, desire, and volition are interwoven in the most variegated patterns. Each lived experience, as filling a moment of our existence, is complex.

The mental system has a teleological character. Wherever the mind learns through pleasure and pain what is valuable, it reacts in attention, selection and elaboration of impressions, in struggle, act of will, choice among its goals, and search for the means to its ends.

So the mere awareness of objects is already clearly purposive. The forms of representing any reality constitute stages in a purposive system, in which the objective element gains ever fuller and more conscious representation. This attitude, in which we apprehend the lived and the given, produces our picture of the world, our concepts of reality, the particular sciences among which the knowledge of this reality is distributed—accordingly, the purposive system of the knowledge of reality. At every stage of this process inclination and feeling are at work. They are the center of our mental structure; from this point all the depths of our being are stirred. We seek an affective state which in some way or other stills our desires. Life is continually approaching this goal. Now life seems to have grasped it; now again the goal recedes. Only the progress of experience teaches each individual what are the enduring values for him. Here the chief work of life is to come through illusions to the knowledge of what is genuinely worth while for us. The system of processes in which we test the values of life and of things, this I call experience of life. It presupposes knowledge of what is, hence our understanding of the objective world. And, as a means to this experience of life, our acts of will, whose immediate purpose concerns changes outside or in ourselves, can serve at the same time for evaluating the elements of our lives as well as external things, in case our interest points to these. Through knowledge of man, through history and poetry, the means to experience of life and the horizon of that experience are enlarged. And in this field also our life can win its security only through elevation to universally valid knowledge. (Can this knowledge, indeed, ever answer the question of absolute value?) The consciousness of life's values is the basis of a third and last system, in which we voluntarily strive to organize and guide movements, men, society, and ourselves. It includes purposes, goods, duties, rules of life, the whole vast business of our practical activity in administration of justice, economy, social regulation, and control over nature. Within this attitude also consciousness advances to higher and higher forms. We seek as the last and highest an activity based on universally valid knowledge, and again the question arises, how far this goal is attainable.

A being which aims somehow at the values of life demanded by the impulses, a being which in its differentiation and integration of activities sets out for this goal, will develop itself. So, from the structure of the inner life its development springs. Every moment and every period of our lives has an intrinsic value insofar as its particular conditions offer for us a definite kind of satisfaction and fulfillment. But, at the same time, all of life's stages are united in a course of development, as we strive in the march of time to achieve a richer and richer unfolding of the values of life, an ever stabler and higher form of inner life. And here also the same basic relation between life and knowledge is shown again; increase of certainty, the raising of our activity to the level of valid, well-grounded knowledge, is essential for our inner stability.

This mental system shows how the empirically established function of philosophy has sprung with inner necessity from the basic properties of mental life. If one imagines an individual as wholly isolated and also free from the temporal restrictions of individual life, this person will apprehend reality, feel values, and achieve goods according to rules of life. A reflective attitude toward his activity must arise in him, and will reach completion only in universally valid knowledge of this activity. And, as apprehension of reality, feeling of values, and realization of goals are interconnected in the depths of this structure, he will strive to grasp the inner system in universally valid knowledge. The elements which cohere deep in the structure—knowledge of the world, experience of life, principles of action—must also be unified somehow in the thinking consciousness. So in this person philosophy arises. It is imbedded in the structure of man. Everyone, whatever his status, is involved in some sort of approach to it, and every human activity tends to reach philosophical reflection.

2. *The Structure of Society and the Position of Religion, Art, and Philosophy in it*

The individual man as an isolated being is a mere abstraction. Blood relationship, community life, competitive and coöperative work, the manifold connections which arise from the common pursuit of goals, and relations of power in dominance and obedience make the individual a member of society. As this society consists of structured individuals, it possesses the same structural regularities. The subjective and immanent purposiveness in individuals manifests itself in history as evolution. The regularities of the individual mind are transformed into those of social life. The differentiation of activities in the individual, with interrelation again at a higher level, assumes stable and effective forms in society as division of labor. The chain of successive generations allows unlimited development, for the products of each kind of work endure as a basis for ever new generations. Intellectual activity spreads out farther and farther, guided by the consciousness of solidarity and of progress. In this way continuity of social work arises, growth of the mental energy expended in it, and increasing organization of the operations involved. These rational elements, active in the life of society and recognized by social psychology, are subject to conditions, upon which the very essence of historical existence rests. Race, climate, circumstances of life, development of classes and political units, personal peculiarities of individuals and groups: these give to every mental product its particular character. But in all of this variety the same purposive systems, which I call systems of culture, arise nevertheless out of the ever constant structure of life, only with various historical modifications. Philosophy can now be defined as one of these cultural systems of human society. For in the coexistence of persons and the sequence of generations those who deal with the riddle of the world and of life through universally valid concepts are united in a purposive system. We must now determine the place of this cultural system in the social economy.

In the knowledge of reality the experiences of successive generations are linked together by the uniformity of our thinking and the identity of the independent world. As this knowledge is thus attained in ever broader scope, it is differentiated in the growing number of particular sciences, and yet remains one through their unifying relation to the one reality and through their common requirement of universally valid knowledge. So, in these particular sciences the culture of our race has its solid, unifying, progressive, guiding basis.

From this great system human culture extends to include all those cultural systems in which acts of will have been integrated and differentiated. For even the voluntary acts of individuals are united in systems which survive the flux of generations. The regularities in the particular spheres of conduct, the constancy of the reality with which this conduct deals, and the demand for coöperative action to realize certain purposes produce the cultural systems of economic life, law, and technology. All this is filled with intrinsic values: joy and enhancement of our existence lie in such activities and are won from them.

But chiefly beyond this tension of will there is an enjoyment of the value of life and of things, in which we relax from the strain. Joy of life, fellowship and festival, sport and jest: that is the atmosphere in which art unfolds, whose very nature is to tarry in a region of free play, where yet the meaning of life is to be seen. Romantic thought has often called attention to the kinship of religion, art, and philosophy. Indeed, the same riddle of the world and of life confronts all three. The religionist, the poet, and the philosopher are related in their attitude toward the social-historical context of their spheres of life: surrounded by this they are still lonely. Their creative activity rises above all environmental orders into a region where, quite alone, they confront the universal powers, above all historical relations to timeless communion with the eternal and omnipresent cause of life. They fear the bonds with which precedents and forms would ensnare their productive activity. They hate the exploitation of personality by the communities whose need measures the honor and worth of their members. So a radical difference separates the encompassing unity in the outer organizations and purposive systems of knowledge or of overt action from the coöperation in the cultural systems of religion, poetry, and philosophy. But freest of all are the poets. Even the fixed relations to reality are dissolved in their play with moods and forms. These common characteristics, which unite religion, poetry, and philosophy, and separate them from the other fields of life, rest ultimately on transcendence of the will's confinement to limited purposes. Man frees himself from this bondage to the given, the determinate, by reflecting upon himself and the unity of things. It is a knowing which is not directed to this or that restricted object, an acting which is not to be completed at any definite place in the purposive system. Perceptual and practical concern with the separate, the spatially and temporally definite, would destroy the wholeness of our being, the consciousness of our intrinsic worth, the awareness that we are independent of the causal chain and of connection with place and time, were there not ever available for man the realm of religion, poetry, and philosophy, in which he finds himself released from such confinement. The contemplations in which he here lives must always somehow encompass the relations of reality, value and ideal, purpose and precept. "Contemplations:" for the creative aspect of religion always lies in a conception of the active system to which the individual is related; poetry is always the representation of an event, grasped in its significance; and the conceptual, systematic method of philosophy obviously expresses the objective attitude. Poetry remains in the region of feeling and contemplation, as it excludes not only every definite purpose, but the volitional attitude itself. In contrast, the awful earnestness of religion and philosophy comes from their aim to fathom the inner continuum which extends in the structure of the mind from the view of reality to the establishment of goals, and from this depth to fashion life. So they become a responsible reflection on life, which is this very totality. Precisely in the full awareness of their truth they come to be zealous forces to form life. Intimately related as they thus are, their common aim to fashion life must breed contention to the point of combat for their existence. Meditation of soul and universal validity of conceptual thought struggle here with each other.

In this way religion, art, and philosophy are, as it were, inserted into the unyielding purposive systems of the particular sciences and social institutions. They stand thus, akin to one another and yet by their mental attitudes estranged from one another, in the most remarkable relations. These we are now to grasp. In other words, we are to see how the urge to a *Weltanschauung* lies in the human mind and how philosophy strives to establish this *Weltanschauung* with universal validity. Then the other side of philosophy will appear, how the concepts and sciences developed in life stimulate the philosophical function of generalization and unification.

II. THEORY OF THE *WELTANSCHAUUNG*. RELIGION AND POETRY IN THEIR RELATIONS TO PHILOSOPHY

Religion, art, and philosophy have in common a basic form, which is rooted in the structure of the inner life. In every moment of our existence there is a persistent relation of our individual lives to the world which surrounds us as a perceptual whole. We feel ourselves, the intrinsic value of the individual moment, and the instrumental value of things to us—this last, however, in relation to the objective world. In the progress of reflection experience of life and development of a world-view go hand in hand. Evaluation of life presupposes knowledge of what exists, and external reality catches variant lights from the inner life. Nothing is more fleeting, frail, and fickle than the mood of man over against the order of nature. Examples of this are those lovely poems which join to a picture of nature the expression of inner life. And, like shadows of clouds which pass over a landscape, perception and evaluation of life and world continually alternate within us. The religious person, the artist, and the philosopher are distinguished from average men—indeed, even from geniuses of another sort—by preserving such moments of life in memory, raising their content to consciousness, and combining the particular experiences into universal experience of life itself. In this way they perform an important function, not only for themselves, but also for society.

Thus at all times interpretations of reality, *Weltanschauungen*, arise. As a sentence expresses its sense or meaning, so these would express the sense and meaning of the world. But yet, after all, how ephemeral are these interpretations in each single individual! Gradually or suddenly they alter under the influence of experiences. As Goethe saw, the periods of human life in typical development adopt various *Weltanschauungen*. Time and place condition their variety. Views of life, artistic expressions of wisdom, religious dogmas, and philosophical formulas cover the earth like a vegetation of countless forms. And like the plants on the ground they seem to be always struggling with one another for existence and room. Now a particular *Weltanschauung*, sustained by the singular greatness of a person, wins power over the people. Saints resolve to imitate the life and death of Christ; long lines of artists see man with the eyes of Raphael; Kant's idealism of freedom sweeps on with it Schiller, Fichte, and indeed most of the influential persons of the following generation. The swirling current of inner events, the fortuitous and particular in the content of life's affairs, the uncertain and shifting in cognition, evaluation, and resolution, this inner misery of the naïve consciousness, so falsely extolled by Rousseau and Nietzsche: these are overcome. The mere form of the religious, artistic, or philosophical attitude brings stability and peace, and creates a bond, uniting the religious genius and the faithful, the master and the pupils, the philosophical personality and those who are subject to its power.

So now the meaning of the riddle of the world and of life, as the common object of religion, philosophy, and poetry, is clarified. A *Weltanschauung* always contains experience of life and view of the world in inner relation, a relation from which an ideal for life can always be derived. Analysis of the greater works in these three creative spheres, and the relation of external reality, value, and moral disposition as the structure of the inner life, lead equally to this insight. Accordingly, a *Weltanschauung* is a systematic whole in which constituent parts of different origin and character are united. The basic difference between these parts goes back to the differentiation of the inner life, which has been called its structure. The application of the term *Weltanschauung* to a creation of mind which includes knowledge of the world, ideals, moral legislation, and choice of ultimate goals is justified, in that a *Weltanschauung* never includes the intention to perform specific acts, hence never a definite practical attitude.

The problem of philosophy's relation to religion and poetry can now be reduced to the question concerning the relations which result from the diverse structures of the *Weltanschauung* in these its three forms. For they enter into essential relations only so far as they each lead to or contain a *Weltanschauung*. As the botanist classifies plants and investigates the laws of their growth, so must the analyst of philosophy hunt for the types of *Weltanschauung* and recognize the regularity in their formation. Such a comparative procedure raises the human mind above the conviction, rooted in its finitude, that in one of these *Weltanschauungen* it has grasped truth itself. As the objectivity of the great historian restrains him from passing judgment on the ideals of particular periods, so through historical comparisons the philosopher must understand the reflective consciousness, which subjects the objective facts to itself, and thus assume his standpoint above them all. Then in him the historical aspect of consciousness is perfected.

The religious *Weltanschauung* is structurally different from the poetic, and the poetic from the philosophical. There is a corresponding difference in the arrangement of the types of *Weltanschauung* within each of these three cultural systems. And the basic differences of the philosophical *Weltanschauung* from the religious and the poetic permit the transition of a *Weltanschauung* from the religious or artistic form into the philosophical, and conversely. The passage into the philosophical form results chiefly from the inner tendency to win practical stability and coherence, goals finally reached only in universally valid thought. So the questions arise: What constitutes the structural individuality of these different forms? According to what relational laws are the religious or artistic transformed into the philosophical? On the threshold of this investigation we approach the general problem for whose treatment there is no room here: the question concerning the relational laws which determine *Weltanschauungen* in their structural variability and diversity of types. Here also the method must be: first to consult historical experience and then to show the mental laws which it exemplifies.

1. *The Religious* Weltanschauung *and its Relations to the Philosophical*

The concept of religion belongs to the same class as the concept of philosophy. It refers first of all to an attitude, common to socially interrelated individuals as a constituent element of their lives. And because this attitude intimately interrelates and systematically unites the individuals who share it, the concept of religion refers also to a system which joins the religious individuals as members of a whole. Here definition encounters the same difficulty as appeared in reference to philosophy. The scope of religious facts would have to be established through a consideration of their affinity and of our use of the term 'religion' to derive the concept of the essence of religion from the facts falling within this scope. The method which resolves these difficulties cannot be presented here. Only its results can be used for the analysis of the religious *Weltanschauung*.

A *Weltanschauung* is religious so far as it has its origin in a definite kind of experience, grounded in a religious event. Wherever the term 'religion' appears, this religion is characterized by communication with the unseen. For such intercourse is present in the primitive stages of religion as well as in those final outgrowths, where the communication consists only in the inner relation of acts to an ideal, which is religious because wholly supernatural, or in the attitude of the mind toward the divine order of things, anthropomorphically conceived. In the history of its forms, religion is developed by this communication into a more and more comprehensive and completely differentiated structure. The process in which this occurs, religious experience, must contain the source of all religious intuitions and the proof of every religious truth. This religious experience is a special form of the experience of life, namely, the reflection accompanying the incidents of communication with the unseen. Experience of life is a reflection, progressing through lived experiences—a reflection on the values of life, the instrumental values of things, and the highest goals and supreme principles of our conduct which issue from these values. Hence, the peculiar feature of religious experience of life is that, where the religious attitude rises to full consciousness, this experience finds the supreme and absolutely authentic value of life in communion with the unseen, and in the invisible object of this communion the supreme and absolutely authentic source of value, that from which all happiness and blessedness flow. So it also follows that this invisible object must determine all goals and rules of action. On this the distinctive element in the structure of the religious *Weltanschauung* depends. It has its center in the lived religious experience, in which the whole of the inner life is active. The cumulative religious experience, grounded in this lived experience, determines every constituent part of the *Weltanschauung*. All views concerning the unity of the world, so far as one considers them in isolation, spring from this communion and must accordingly interpret this unity as a power, standing in relation to our lives, and, to be sure, as a mental power, since only a power of this sort makes such communion possible. The religious relation must determine the ideal of life, that is, the inner hierarchy of its values, and, finally, must yield the supreme principle for human relations.

The various ways in which this religious communication can occur distinguish the historical stages and forms in which the religious *Weltanschauung* develops.

In the earliest known expressions of the religious attitude, we find a belief and a practice constantly joined. They presuppose each other. For, however the belief in living, willing, active forces around men may have arisen, we find the development of this belief, as far as we can trace it in ethnology and history, shown by the way in which religious objects take on form precisely through action toward them. And, conversely, belief in turn determines ritual, since in belief religious activity first receives its goal. To primitive peoples religion is the technique of influencing the inscrutable, the inaccessible to merely mechanical change, of assimilating its powers, of uniting oneself with it, of securing a desired relation to it. Such religious activities are perfected by an individual, the chief or the magician-priest. So a vocational class grows up for their administration. At the beginning of every differentiation of masculine vocations this profession of the magician, medicine man, or priest arises— a profession uncanny, none too highly respected, yet regarded with an awe, now fearful, now expectant. It gradually grows into an organized class, which carries on all religious communication, and techniques of magic, expiation, and purification. This class remains the proprietor of knowledge, until an autonomous science breaks away. Through asceticism these men must free themselves for the gods. Through renunciations, separating them in their holiness and worth from all other persons, they must prove their relation to the unseen. That is the first, restricted form in which the religious ideal appears.

Out of this communication with the unseen, carried on by special persons for the attainment of goods and prevention of evils, primitive religious ideas develop at this level of the religious attitude. They rest on myth-making imagination and its conformity to psychological laws. It is already implicit in the original vitality and wholeness of man that in all of his relations to the outer world he discovers expressions of something living, and that is the universal assumption of religious intercourse. The performance of religious acts inevitably strengthens this form of interpretation. Subjective, changing, various as these practical beliefs are, yet in every nomadic horde or tribe they remain similar through the common presence of religious experience, whose peculiar logic of analogy enables them to win certainty. Where still no comparison with scientific evidence is made, such certainty and agreement can much more easily grow up. Where dreams, visions, and abnormal nervous states of every sort enter daily life as miracles, they furnish religious logic with empirical content singularly suited to verify influences of the unseen. The suggestive power of the beliefs, their mutual confirmation, which follows the same religious logic as their first establishment, then the quasi-experimental verification afforded by the demonstrated efficacy of a fetish or of a sorcerer's manipulation (just as we today see the power of a shrine proved by the sick and established on the evidence of pictures and reports from places of pilgrimage), then also the actions of magicians, oracle-priests, and monks, violent movements and extraordinary states with appearances and revelations, called forth by fasting, noisy music, intoxication of some sort: all that strengthens the religious kind of certainty. But the essential fact is, nevertheless, that in the first cultural stages, known to us, religious belief, in accordance with the nature of the men of that time and their conditions of life, uses impressive experiences of birth, death, sickness, visions, and madness for its primitive religious ideas, which are therefore to be found everywhere in like form. In every living, animate body dwells a second I, the soul (thought of also, perhaps, as a plurality) which leaves the body temporarily in life, permanently in death, and in its shadowy existence is capable of various activities. The whole of nature is alive with spiritual beings, which influence man, and which he strives to dispose favorably through magic, sacrifice, ceremonial worship, and prayer. Heaven, sun, and stars are seats of divine forces. (Here let us merely point to another group of ideas which arises in peoples of a lower grade and concerns the origin of men or the world.)

These primitive ideas form the basis of the religious *Weltanschauung*. They are remolded and coalesce, every change in the state of culture affecting this development. Within the gradual transformation of the religious attitude the decisive factor for the advance to a *Weltanschauung* is the change in the nature of this communication with the unseen. Beyond the official form of worship with its temples, sacrifices, and ceremonies a freer, esoteric relation of the soul to the divine arises. A group of men, distinguished by greater religious cultivation, enters into this peculiar relation to deity, secluding itself therein or also allowing others to enter. In mysteries, in hermitic life, and in prophecy the new relation gains authority. The religious genius reveals the mysterious power of personality to achieve integration in comprehending the world, evaluating life, and organizing its affairs. Religious experiences and their resultant ideas enter, as it were, into another pattern. The relation of the religious persons to those whom they influence takes on a different inner form. Particular effects are not experienced or sought, but the whole mind enters into this inner communion. These great personalities cease to be subject to inscrutable, obscure forces, rejoicing and suffering in the secret consciousness of the abuse and corruption of these forces. The danger, lurking in this new, purer relation, is defferent: the enhancement of self-consciousness, which springs from their influence on the believers, and from communion with the unseen derives the character of a peculiar relation to this hidden being. But, among the virtues which emerge from the new relation, one of the strongest is that it prepares the way for a unitary *Weltanschauung* through the inner connection in which all aspects of religious communion and all sides of its object merge. Wherever capacities and circumstances permit a normal growth, a religious *Weltanschauung* is formed, no matter how long a time is needed for this change at the various places of progress toward it, no matter what stages are traversed, or whether the names of the religious personalities are forgotten.

Structure and content of the religious *Weltanschauung*, as it evolves in this way, are determined by religious communion and the experience developing in it. And hence the primitive ideas maintain their strength with unusual tenacity in spite of continual transformation. Thus in religion world-views, evaluations, and ideals of life receive their peculiar form and color.

In these experiences of religious communication man finds himself determined by something dynamic, inscrutable, and uncontrollable within the causal nexus of nature. It is purposive and psychical. Thus the basic form of the religious view arises, as it gains currency in myth, ceremonial activity, worship of sensory objects, and allegorical exegesis of sacred scriptures. The method of religious vision and confirmation, which rests on belief in souls and worship of stars and is developed in primitive communication with the unseen, here reaches the inner coherence adequate to the stage of the *Weltanschauung*. The understanding cannot comprehend, but only distinguish, the assumptions seen to be implicit in this method. Here the particular and visible signifies something which is more than that in which it appears. This relation is distinct from the signification of signs, the meaning in judgment, the symbolism in art, and yet akin to them. It contains a representation of a very peculiar kind, for everything apparent and visible merely signifies the unseen and yet is identical with it. That is the relation of the visible world to deity. Therein is the effective power of the unseen. Consequently, even at this stage of inner communion with the unseen, its illumination of the visible particular, its action there, and the divine revelation of itself in persons and religious deeds persists. And even the unification of deities, connected with this stage, has been able only in a minority of peoples and religions to overcome permanently this feature of the religious view. In various ways from early times divine powers have been merged in a highest. This transition had been effected about 600 B.C. in the most important peoples of the Orient. The unity of names, the sovereignty of the god proved strongest by victory, the uniqueness of the holy, the resolution of all differences in the mystical religious object, insight into the harmonious order of the stars: these and other starting points, all quite different, led to the doctrine of the One Unseen. And, as in the centuries of this vast movement among the oriental peoples very active intercourse among them continued, this undoubtedly helped to propagate the greatest idea of these times. But each of these intuitions of the world-conditioning unity shows the marks of its religious origin in its inclusion of goodness, provident insight, and relevance to human needs. And in most of them the basic category of religious understanding portrays the divine as surrounded by forces which lie in the visible world. Or it must appear as God on the earth; it struggles with demoniacal powers; it shows itself in holy places or in miracles; it operates in ceremonial activities. Religious language concerning divinity must always be both sensory and spiritual. Symbols like light, purity, and height express the values felt to be in the divine being. The most general, definitive, and tenable scheme of interpretation for the divinely conditioned coherence of things is the teleological constitution of the world. Behind the nexus of external objects, in it and over it, stands a spiritual order, in which divine purpose manifests itself. At this point the religious *Weltanschauung* passes over into the philosophical, for metaphysical thought from Anaxagoras to Thomas and Duns Scotus has been determined chiefly by the concept of teleological world-order.

In inward communion with the unseen the naïve consciousness of life undergoes a conversion. The more the face of the religious genius is turned to the other world and his soul is absorbed in the relationship, the more this yearning consumes all worldly values, so far as they do not minister to the communion with God. Thus the ideal of the saint arises and the ascetic technique, which seeks to destroy the ephemeral, covetous, and sensual in the individual. Conceptual thought cannot express this conversion from the sensual to the divine. In the symbolic language common to quite different religions it is called rebirth, and its goal the human soul's communion of love with the divine being.

In the sphere of conduct and institutions a new component, in addition to the consecration of secular relations, grows out of religious communion. All who commune with deity are thereby united in a community, and this is as superior to every other as the religious relation outweighs other institutions in value. The inner depth and strength of the bonds in this community have found appropriate expression in the symbolic language of religion: the members are called children of God and brothers.

This character of the religions *Weltanschauung* explains its chief types and their mutual bearings: evolution of the universe; immanence of the world-reason in the social order and the course of nature; behind all division a spiritual All-One, to which the soul surrenders its own being; the duality of the good, pure, divine order and the demoniacal; the ethical monotheism of freedom. These basic types of the religious *Weltanschauung* all comprehend deity through value-relations which religious intercourse establishes between the human and the divine, the sensual and the ethical, plurality and unity, the social order and the religious good. We can recognize them as the pre-stages of the philosophical *Weltanschauungen* into which they pass over. In all peoples which have progressed to or toward philosophy it is preceded by religion and mysticism.

This change is connected with a more general one, which takes place in the form of the religious *Weltanschauung*. Religious ideas again pass into another pattern. Religion and the religious *Weltanschauung* are converted gradually—for all these changes are slow—into the conceptual form without displacing the intuitive. But although the inferior kinds of religious intercourse remain beside the higher, they survive in every more developed religion as its lower strata. Magic in religious ritual, subjection to the priests endowed with magic power, and the crudest sensory belief in the efficacy of religious places and images linger on in the same religion, in the same creed, with deep mysticism growing out of the purest inwardness of religious communion. In the same way the hieroglyphics of religious symbolism still retain their value beside the conceptual forms of theology. But, though the stages of religious intercourse are related to one another as higher and lower, such a relation does not obtain between the various forms of the religious *Weltanschauung*. For it lies, of course, in the nature of all religious experiences to seek assurance of their objective validity, and only in conceptual thought can that goal be reached. Yet this very conceptual labor reveals their total inadequacy for such an undertaking.

These processes can be studied most thoroughly in the religious attitudes of India and Christianity. In the Vedanta-philosophy and in the philosophy of Albertus and Thomas such a change was realized. But in both cases it proved impossible to surmount the inner barrier rooted in the peculiar nature of the religious attitude. This attitude (which, in turn, had its presuppositions in an older set of dogmas) gave rise to the intuition of escape from the chain of birth, work, recompense, and exploration of knowledge, in which the soul comprehends its identity with Brahma. Thus the contradiction developed between the dreadful reality, in which dogma included the inevitable circle of doer, deed, and suffering, and the illusory nature of everything particular, which metaphysical doctrine demanded. Christianity was originally presented in dogmas of the first order: the creation, fall of man, revelation of God, union of Christ with God, redemption, sacrifice, and atonement. These religious symbols and their mutual relation belong to an utterly different region from that of the understanding. But an inner need now drove thought on to clarify the content of these dogmas and to bring out their implicit vision of things divine and human. One does the history of Christianity an injustice in regarding its adoption of Graeco-Roman philosophical principles as merely an external fate, imposed by its environment. It was also an inner necessity, inherent in the constitutive laws of the religious attitude itself. Then in the adaptation of the first dogmas to the cosmological categories the dogmas of the second order arose: the doctrine of the attributes of God, of the nature of Christ, of the process of the Christian life in man. And here the inwardness of the Christian religion suffered a tragic fate. These concepts isolated and contrasted the elements of life. In this way the irresolvable conflict arose between God's infinitude and His attributes, between these interrelated attributes, between the divine and human in Christ, between freedom of will and predestination, between our ethical nature and the atonement through the sacrifice of Christ. Scholasticism labored away at these antinomies in vain; rationalism used them to dispose of dogma;

mysticism returned to an extreme doctrine of religious certainty. And though from Albertus scholasticism was led on to transmute the religious into a philosophical *Weltanschauung* and to free this from the alien sphere of positive dogmas, yet even so it could not overcome the restrictions which were imposed by Christian communion with God. The divine attributes, posited in this communion, remained incompatible with God's infinitude, and His determination of man with man's freedom. The same impossibility of changing the religious into the philosophical *Weltanschauung* appeared wherever this attempt was made. Philosophy arose in Greece, where wholly independent persons aimed directly at universally valid knowledge of the world. And philosophy was reëstablished in modern nations by investigators who independently of the ecclesiastical orders, set themselves the same problem of world-knowledge. Arising both times in connection with the sciences, it rested on the establishment of this world-knowledge in a fixed frame of causal connections, in opposition to the world-evaluations of religion. With philosophy an altered attitude of mind gains prevalence.

This analysis shows in what respects the religious and philosophical *Weltanschauungen* are similar, and in what respects they differ. In broad outline they have the same structure. Cognition, evaluation, resolution, and regulation have the same necessary relation in both. There is the same inner systematic unity, in which personality is gathered up into itself and secured. For this very reason knowledge of the objective world contains the power to fashion personal life and the social order. So close, so akin are these *Weltanschauungen* to each other, so agreed with respect to the field they aim to govern, that they must always collide. For their relations to the riddle of the world and of life, as it lies thus spread out before them both, are nevertheless utterly different—as different as religious intercourse and the broad relation to all kinds of reality, as different as the self-certain religious experience, steadfast in its aim, and an experience of life which reflects impartially and calmly upon every inner act and attitude. In religion the great lived experience of an absolute, infinite, objective value, to which all finite values are subordinate, of the infinite personal value of communion with this unseen object determines the whole view of visible objects and choice of objectives. Indeed, man's transcendent consciousness of a spiritual being is itself only the projection of the greatest religious experience, in which he realizes that his will is independent of the whole natural order. This origin of the religious *Weltanschauung* colors every one of its features. The basic form of vision and confirmation, imposed by this origin, controls—secretly, dangerously, and irresistably—every religious creation. In philosophy, on the other hand, there is a restful balance of mental attitudes, a recognition of what each of them yields, accordingly a use of the particular sciences and a joy in secular institutions. But there is also incessant labor to discover a universally valid coherence in all this, and an ever growing experience of the limits of knowledge, of the impossibility of combining objectively what is given in the various attitudes—hence, resignation.

Thus the historical relations arise between these two kinds of *Weltanschauung*, which have been established in terminology, definition, and historical fact. The religious attitude is subjective and determined by particular lived experiences. An inexplicable, supremely personal element is present, which must seem absurd to anyone who does not share these experiences. This attitude remains confined to the limits inherent in its origin in one-sided, historically and personally conditioned religious experience, and inherent also in the inner form of religious intuition and the nisus to the transcendent. But now, as the religious attitude in its cultural context encounters scientific results, conceptual thinking, and secular education, it comes to see its vulnerability in all its inner power, its limitations in every claim to communication and influence abroad. The religious man who feels deeply enough to perceive these barriers and be troubled must strive to surmount them. The mental law, that general ideas can be completed only in conceptual thought, forces him into the same course. The religious *Weltanschauung* strives to become philosophical.

But, nevertheless, the other side of this historical relation lies in the fact that the religious *Weltanschauung* in its conceptual presentation and its logical grounding has afforded extensive preparation for the philosophical. First, the attempts to derive religious knowledge from principles were very fruitful for philosophy. Whatever the facts concerning the originality of Augustine in regard to the propositions passed on to Descartes, still from Augustine came the stimulus for the new epistemological method. Tenets of another kind went from mysticism to Nicholas of Cusa and thence to Bruno, and Descartes and Leibniz were influenced by Albertus and Thomas in their distinction between eternal truths and the order of facts, which is intelligible only in terms of purpose. Also we are seeing more and more how extensively the logical and metaphysical concepts of the scholastics affected Descartes, Spinoza, and Leibniz. And the types of religious and of philosophical *Weltanschauung* stand in various relations to each other. The realism of a good and an evil realm, which the religious attitude of Zarathustra transmitted to that of Judaism and Christianity, was involved in the analysis of reality in terms of formative power and matter, thus imparting a peculiar tinge to Platonism. The doctrine of the evolution from the lower to the higher divine beings, as it appeared in Babylonia and Greece, paved the way for the doctrine of the evolution of the world. The Chinese teaching of the spiritual order in nature and the Indian teaching of the illusion and suffering of sensory multiplicity and the truth and blessedness of unity helped to determine both of the directions in which objective idealism was to unfold. Finally, the Israelitic and Christian belief in the transcendence of a holy creator prepared for that type of philosophical *Weltanschauung* which has spread most widely in the Christian as in the Mohammedan world. Thus, the types of religious *Weltanschauung* have all influenced the philosophical, but especially they contain the basis for two types: objective idealism and the idealism of freedom. The doctrine of *gnosis* created the schema for the most influential pantheistic works: emanation of the multifarious world; the beauty and power in it, but also the suffering of finitude and separation; return into the divine unity. The Neo-Platonists, Spinoza, and Schopenhauer have developed it into a philosophy. And the *Weltanschauung* of Christianity, the idealism of freedom, first opened up theological problems and their solutions, which then influenced Descartes as well as Kant. So we understand why and where the religious authors must find a place in the historical continuity of philosophy, and could even be called philosophers. Yet we also see clearly how no writing, determined by the religious attitude, may claim a position in the whole system of philosophy, where the possibilities of the universally valid solution of philosophical problems have evolved in an inner logical dialectic.

2. *Philosophy and the Life-View of the Poets*

In something particular and set off within bounds every art enables one to see relations transcending this particular object and thus giving it a more general significance. The impression of sublimity, which the figures of Michelangelo or the compositions of Beethoven produce, springs from the peculiar character of the meaning embodied in these works of art, and this presupposes a firm, strong, constant, integrated personality, subordinating to itself whatever confronts it. But only one art is equipped to express more than such a mental constitution. All other arts are confined to the effective presentation of a sensory object; herein lies their strength and their limitation. Poetry alone deals freely with the whole realm of reality and of ideas. For in language it is able to express whatever can appear in the mind of men—external objects, inner states, values, decisions—and this language, its means of expression, already involves the grasp of the given through thought. Therefore, if anywhere in works of art a *Weltanschauung* is expressed, it is in poetry.

I am attempting so to treat the questions arising here as to obviate the need of referring to the differences within the aesthetic and psychological standpoints. All poetic works, from the most fugitive folksong to the *Orestes* of Aeschylus or Goethe's *Faust*, agree in this, that they represent an event, this word taken to include experiences, possible and actual, our own and others', past and present. The representation of an event in poetry is the fictitious appearance of a reality, relived and offered for reliving, lifted out of the context of existence and our relations of will and interest. So it evokes no overt response. Events which would otherwise incite the observer to action no longer stir his passive attitude. They produce no inhibition and no impulse. As long as one tarries in the region of art, all pressure of reality is taken from his mind. If a lived experience is lifted into this world of appearance, the processes which it evokes in the reader or listener are not the same as they were in the persons living it. In order to grasp these original processes more exactly we distinguish here between the processes of reliving and those which accompany, as effects, our grasp of the other person's lived experience. The stream of consciousness in which I catch Cordelia's emotions and tensions of will is different from the admiration and sympathy which spring from this reliving. Then, the mere understanding of a story or a play includes further processes, which transcend those taking place in the characters of the plot. The reader of a poetic narrative must relate subject to predicate, sentence to sentence, outer to inner, motives to deeds and these to consequences, to be able to change the words of the report into the picture of the event, and this into the inner system of lived experience. To understand the factual content he must subordinate it to the general ideas and relations implicit in the words. And the more the reader is absorbed in this event, the more his processes of recollection, apperception, and relation pass beyond what the poet has expressed in the narrative to something which he did not say, but may have wished to evoke in the reader precisely through what he did express. Perhaps that concerned him more than what he said. In what is recounted the reader sees the general features of a life-situation, through which the story is understood. So the spectator of a drama supplements what he sees and hears on the stage to form a more inclusive whole. The way in which the plot subjects human deeds to the judgment of fate reveals to him an aspect of life. He relates himself to what goes on there as to life itself. He interprets the particular in its context or as a case of a general situation. And, without his needing to note it, in this process the poet is his guide, letting him draw from the incident portrayed something transcending it. Thus we see that epic as well as dramatic poetry so represents an event for the reader, hearer, or spectator that its significance is grasped. For an event is grasped as significant so far as it reveals to us something of the nature of life. Poetry is the organ of the understanding of life; the poet is a seer who discerns life's meaning. And here the interpreter's understanding and the poet's creating meet. For this creating is the mysterious process of heating the hard, jagged, crude ore of a lived experience and recasting it in that form significant for the interpreter. Shakespeare reads in his Plutarch the biographies of Caesar and Brutus. He combines them in his picture of the events. Now the characters of Caesar, Brutus, Cassius, and Antony provide mutual illumination; there is a necessity in their attitudes toward one another. And when among these great personalities the heads of the greedy, thoughtless, servile mass become visible, one sees clearly the inevitable end of the fateful conflict between the principals. The poet knows Elizabeth, the royal character of Henry the Fifth, and other kings of many kinds. He discovers an essential feature of human affairs, which renders all the facts of Plutarch coherent, and explains the historical event as a particular case: the triumph of the unscrupulous, dominant nature, master of reality, over the republican ideals with no more champions. So understood, felt, and generalized, this life-situation becomes for him the motif of a tragedy. For a motif is precisely a life-situation, poetically understood in its significance. And now in this motif an inner motive power operates so to adapt characters, events, and actions to one another as to show that general feature in the nature of things without the poet's expressing it, or even so much as being able to express it. For every general feature of life is related to the meaning of life as such, hence to something wholly inscrutable.

So we have now answered the question, how far the poet expresses a view of life or even a *Weltanschauung*. Every lyric, epic, or dramatic poem lifts a particular experience to the level of reflection on its significance. In this such a poem is distinguished from the entertaining, machine-made verse. It has every device to let this significance be seen without explicitly stating it. And the demand that the meaning of the event be expressed in the inner form of the poem must certainly be met in every case. As a rule, the poem then somehow proceeds to give also a general expression to the significance of what occurs. Some of the most beautiful lyric poems and folksongs often express the feeling of the situation simply, but still the most profound effect arises, when the feeling spreads out in a regular expansion and dies away in the consciousness of its significance. In Dante and Goethe this procedure borders on philosophical poetry. In stories the action seems suddenly to stop as the light of thought falls on it, or conversation illumines the meaning of what is happening, as in the wise words of Don Quixote, Meister, and Lothario. In the middle of a drama's stormy course the reflection of the characters on themselves and the events appears and releases the mind of the spectator. Indeed, many great poems go a step further still. In conversation, monologue, or chorus they combine the ideas about life, as they emerge from the events, to form a coherent and universal interpretation of life. Greek tragedy, Schiller's *Bride of Messina*, and Hölderlin's *Death of Empedocles* are outstanding examples of this.

On the other hand, poetry leaves its proper realm whenever, detached from lived experience, it undertakes to express thoughts about the nature of things. Then an intermediate form arises between poetry and philosophy or description of nature, and its effect is entirely different from that of really poetic works. Schiller's *Gods of Greece*, the gods being ideals in the form of lived experiences, which run their courses according to the laws of feeling, is true, inner, lyric poetry. But other famous poems of Lucretius, Haller, and Schiller belong to the intermediate class, because they endow a product of thought with values of feeling and cloak it with images of fantasy. This intermediate form has justified itself by its great effects, but it is not pure poetry.

Through its content, the particular lived experience, all genuine poetry is bound up with what the poet discovers in himself, in others, and in the various records of human events. Experience of life is the living spring whence flows poetic knowledge of the significance of these events. This significance is much more than a value recognized in an event. For the structure of the inner life makes its causal system identical with its teleological nature, as seen in a persistent urge to produce intrinsic values and in a steady, vital relation to instrumental values of every kind. Hence the poet draws from experience of life, and he broadens its previous content, whenever, more acutely than before, he sees signs of something inward, or notices anew a blend of traits in a character, whenever he first observes a peculiar relation resulting from the nature of two characters—in short, whenever he sees a nuance of life. Out of such elements an inner world is constructed. He traces the history of the passions and the development of widely different men. He organizes the world of characters according to kinship, diversity, and types. All this enters a complex, higher form, when he grasps inclusive, universal features in the individual or in social-historical life. And still his understanding of life has not reached its peak. His work will be so much the more mature, the more the motif, which consists in such a trend of life, is raised into relation with the whole system of life. Then it is seen within its bounds, and yet at the same time in the highest ideal relations. Every great poet must experience this advance in himself, as it leads him on out of the one-sided strength of *Intrigue and Love* or from the first fragments of *Faust* to *Wallenstein* and to Goethe's later work.

This reflection on the meaning of life can find an adequate foundation only in the knowledge of things divine and human, and its conclusion only in an ideal for the conduct of life. So it tends toward a *Weltanschauung*. The theory of life, philosophy, and the sciences around him come to the aid of this inner urge in the poet. But, whatever he may also adopt from them, the origin of his *Weltanschauung* gives it a characteristic structure. In distinction from the religious *Weltanschauung* it is impartial, universal, and insatiable in assimilating all reality. Its objective view of nature and of the ultimate interconnection of things is always for the sake of penetrating deeply into the significance of life, and this very significance gives freedom and vitality to its ideals. The philosopher is so much the more scientific, the more he neatly separates kinds of attitude and analyses intuition; the poet creates from the totality of his powers.

If ability and environment lead a poet to develop a *Weltanschauung*, still it can only to a limited extent be read immediately from a particular work. It stands out most effectively not in direct expression, which is never exhaustive, but in the power to combine the manifold in a unity, the parts in an organized whole. Even to the melody of the verse, to the rhythm of the emotional sequence, the inner form of every genuine poem is determined by the conscious attitude of the poet and his age. The types of technique in every kind of poetry must be understood as the expression of various individual, historical ways of interpreting life. But as thus a body arises, whose soul is a trend of life, thrown into relief by an event, in this body the *Weltanschauung* of the poet can appear but partially; it is whole only in the poet himself. Hence, the supreme effect of the truly great poet first appears when one advances to the coherence of the aspects of life portrayed in the particular works. When *Torquato Tasso* and *Iphigenia* followed Goethe's first vigorous poems they had only a moderate effect on a limited number of persons. But then, as the Schlegels and their romantic companions showed the inner connection of these poems in a personal attitude and the relevance of the style to this, it enhanced Goethe's influence. So little justified is the vulgar prejudice that works of art are rendered less effective by an understanding derived from aesthetics or the history of literature.

The forms of poetic *Weltanschauung* are infinitely various and flexible. What his period contributes to the poet and what he produces from his experience of life combine to impose, from without, firm bonds and barriers upon his thinking. But the inner urge to explain life from experience of life presses constantly against these barriers. Even where a poet receives the systematic frame of his thought from without, like Dante, Calderón, or Schiller, still the power of transformation is ever restless within him. But the more freely he draws from the experience of life, the more he is subject to the power of life, which is always presenting new aspects to him. So the history of poetry reveals the endless possibilities of feeling and perceiving life, which are contained in human nature and its relations to the world. The religious relation, which forms communities and creates tradition, and the character of philosophical thinking, which is expressed in the continuity of stable, conceptual structures, tend to limit the *Weltanschauung* to fixed types. The poet is the true man even in his free surrender of himself to the action of life upon him. The common man's reflection on life is too weak for him to reach a secure position in the modern anarchy of views of life. In the poet the effect of the various aspects of life is too strong, and his sensitivity to its nuances is too great, for one definite type of *Weltanschauung* always to express adequately what life tells him.

The history of poetry shows the growth of the effort and the ability to understand life in terms of itself. In the particular nation and also in mankind as a whole the influence of the religious *Weltanschauung* on the poet is steadily ebbing; more and more the effect of scientific thinking is felt. The mutual struggle of *Weltanschauungen* absorbs from each of them ever more of its power over the people. In highly cultivated nations the discipline of thought is steadily reducing the strength of fantasy. So it is becoming almost a rule of method for the poets to interpret the reality of things without prejudice. And every present poetic tendency is seeking to perform this task, each in its own way.

These characteristics of the poetic view of life and *Weltanschauung* create the historical relation of poetry to philosophy. The structure of these poetic views is quite unlike the conceptual articulation of the philosophical *Weltanschauung*. No regular advance from the former to the latter is possible. There are no concepts which could be taken up and elaborated. Nevertheless, poetry affects philosophical thinking. Poetry paved the way for the origin of philosophy in Greece and its renewal in the Renaissance. It exerts a regular, steadily persistent influence on the philosophers. First within itself poetry cultivated an objective consideration of the world-order, entirely divorced from interest and utility, thus preparing for the philosophical attitude. The effect of Homer in this respect must have been enormous. His work was a model for the free movement of the observing eye over the whole breadth of the world's life. His insights into man became inexhaustible material for psychological analysis. He expressed the ideal of a higher humanity more freely, clearly, and humanely than philosophy could at that time. His view of life and *Weltanschauung* determined the personal attitudes of great philosophers. In philosophy, from Bruno on, the new joy of the Renaissance artists in life became the doctrine of the immanence of values in the world. Goethe's *Faust* contained a new concept of the universal power of man to enter into the whole in contemplation, enjoyment, and action. And so, beside the ideal of the transcendental school, he exerted a philosophical influence on the elevation of human existence. Schiller's historical dramas strongly affected the development of the historical consciousness. The poetic pantheism in Goethe prepared the way for the maturation of the philosophical. And how the influence of philosophy permeates all poetry, penetrating into its most central concern, the development of a view of life! Philosophy offers its finished concepts, its definitive types of world-view. It ensnares poetry—dangerously and yet indispensably. Euripides studied the Sophists, Dante the medieval thinkers and Aristotle. Racine came from Port-Royal, Diderot and Lessing from the philosophy of the Enlightenment. Goethe plunged into Spinoza and Schiller became the pupil of Kant. And even if Shakespeare, Cervantes, and Molière surrendered to no philosophy, yet countless subtle influences of philosophical doctrines pervade their works as their indispensable means of holding fast the aspects of life.

III. The Philosophical *WELTANSCHAUUNG*.
The Attempt to Raise the *WELTANSCHAUUNG* To Universal Validity

Thus the tendency to develop a view of life and a *Weltanschauung* joins religion, poetry, and philosophy. In these historical relations philosophy has evolved with the further urge from the beginning to make this view of life and *Weltanschauung* universally valid. Wherever in various regions of Eastern culture the development through the religious *Weltanschauung* to the philosophical began, this urge alone remained dominant, and all other philosophical activity subordinate to it. Then, when full-fledged philosophy appeared in Greece, the same urge in the old Pythagorean school and in Heraclitus succeeded in embracing all existence in a *Weltanschauung*. And this attempt governed the whole further development of philosophy for more than two thousand years until the era of Locke, the *New Essays* of Leibniz, and Berkeley in a sequence, starting at the end of the seventeenth century. To be sure, during this period philosophy had to combat the empirical understanding, the men of the world, and the positive investigators. But that was an opposition which made itself felt from without, as it were, against the philosophical urge. The scepticism which issued from within philosophy itself, from reflection on the methods and scope of knowledge, had the heart of its problem precisely in its relation to the same ineradicable need of the mind. The negativity of the sceptical attitude in the face of this need proved its state of mind to be unrealistic. And we have seen how, even in the two centuries which advanced the work of Locke, Leibniz, and Berkeley, a deep concern with the problem of a universally valid *Weltanschauung* persisted. Quite the greatest thinker of these two centuries, Kant, is most deeply concerned.

The central position of the *Weltanschauung* in philosophy can be established also through the relation of philosophy to both of the other historical forces. The centrality of the *Weltanschauung* in turn explains the fact that the religious attitude has lived in ceaseless struggle with philosophy, and that poetry, which has given so much to philosophy and received so much from it, could hold its ground only in constantly contesting the claims of the abstract interpretation of life to dominance. Was Hegel perhaps right in asserting that the religious attitude and art are subordinate forms in the unfolding of the essence of philosophy, forms destined to transmute themselves more and more into the higher mode of consciousness proper to the philosophical *Weltanschauung*? The answer to this question depends chiefly upon whether the desire for a scientifically grounded world-view ever reaches its goal.

1. *The Structure of the Philosophical* Weltanschauung

The philosophical *Weltanschauung* with its original tendency to universal validity must be essentially different in structure from the religious and the poetical. In distinction from the religious it is universal and universally valid; in distinction from the poetic it is a power which seeks to reform life. It develops on the broadest foundation, the empirical consciousness (experience and the sciences of experience), according to the formative laws involved when lived experiences are objectified in conceptual thought. Since the power of discursive, judgmental thought, which always refers a statement to an object, penetrates all the depths of lived experiences, the whole world of feeling and volition is objectified as concepts of value and their relations, and as laws of obligation. The kinds of object, corresponding to the modes of attitude, are distinguished. In every sphere, defined by a basic attitude, a systematic structure is formed. The relations of implication, which hold between statements, require a fixed standard of evidence for knowledge of existence. In the region of values this very situation brings about an advance of thought to postulates concerning objective values, indeed, to the claim of an absolute value. And so in the field of conduct thought comes to rest only when it has reached a highest good or a supreme principle. The elements which constitute life thus dispose themselves for systems through the generalization of concepts and propositions. Logical grounding, as the form of systematic thinking, links the conceptual members in each of these systems ever more clearly and completely. And the highest concepts to which the systems attain—universal being, ultimate ground, absolute value, highest good—are combined in the concept of a teleological world-order, in which philosophy agrees with the religious attitude and artistic thought. Thus, in accordance with formative laws of the mind the basic features of the teleological pattern of world-view have arisen. And so, in fact, this pattern was permanently established until the close of the Middle Ages, and its natural power till the present day. On its basis or in opposition to it the fundamental forms of philosophical *Weltanschauung* have diverged.

When the *Weltanschauung* is grasped conceptually, grounded in principles, and thus raised to universal validity, we call it metaphysics. It expands into a variety of forms. Individuality, circumstances, nation, and period evoke countless nuances of world-view from the philosophers as from the poets. For the structure of our inner life may be affected by the world in infinitely many ways. And likewise the means of thought vary continually with the state of the scientific mind. But from the fact that processes of thought are continuous, and that knowledge of a certain kind characterizes philosophy, it follows that the groups of systems have an inner coherence, and that different thinkers feel both a mutual affinity and an opposition to other groups. Thus in classical Greek philosophy opposition appeared between teleological metaphysics—as it were, the natural metaphysical system—and the *Weltanschauung* which restricts knowledge of the world to causal explanation. Then, as the significance of the problem of freedom came to be recognized from Stoicism on, the systems of objective idealism, in which the ground of things determines the world-order, diverged more and more clearly from the idealistic systems of freedom, in which the lived experience of free will is held fast and projected into the world-ground itself. Basic types of metaphysics developed, rooted in the decisive differences of human *Weltanschauungen*. They cover a great variety of these *Weltanschauungen* and of systematic forms.

2. *Types of Philosophical* Weltanschauung

The historical induction needed to establish these types cannot be presented here. The empirical characteristics from which this induction proceeds lie in the essential kinship of metaphysical systems, in their relations of causal connection and transformation, in the recognition by thinkers of their affinity and their opposition. But, above all, we find these characteristics in the inner historical continuity in which such a type grows clearer and clearer and is grounded ever more deeply, and in the influence of such typical systems as those of Spinoza, Leibniz, or Hegel, of Kant or Fichte, of d'Alembert, Hobbes, or Comte. Between these types there are forms in which the *Weltanschau-*

ungen are not yet clearly distinguished. Other forms, defying consistency of thought, would cling to the whole group of metaphysical motifs. These always prove to be unfruitful for the further development of the *Weltanschauung* and ineffective in life and literature, however strong they may be in virtue of their complicated ground-plan or technical advantages. From the motley variety of such nuances in the *Weltanschauung* the consistent, pure, highly influential types stand out significantly. From Democritus, Lucretius, and Epicurus to Hobbes, from Hobbes to the Encyclopedists and to modern materialism as well as to Comte and Avenarius, in spite of the great diversity of the systems, a continuity can still be traced, which joins these groups of systems in a unitary type, whose first form can be called materialistic or naturalistic and whose further development under the influence of the critical consciousness logically leads to Comtean positivism. Heraclitus, strict Stoicism, Spinoza, Leibniz, Shaftesbury, Goethe, Schelling, Schleiermacher, and Hegel mark the stages of objective idealism. Plato, the Hellenistic-Roman philosophy of life, which Cicero represents, Christian speculation, Kant, Fichte, Maine de Biran with the French thinkers related to him, and Carlyle form the developmental stages of the idealism of freedom. The inner regularity which we saw in the formation of metaphysical systems differentiates them into these orders. This development and the modifications appearing in it are affected chiefly by the process we have set forth, in which the relation to reality passes through definite positions. So positivism confronted us earlier as the most striking case of the non-metaphysical method which seeks a firm ground for knowledge, while now in its totality it is regarded as a form of *Weltanschauung*, epistemologically grounded in this method. But, then, the development and finer discrimination of types depends on the growth of human ideals from the relations of values, goals, and obligations.

The knowledge of objective reality is based on the study of nature, for this alone can win a lawful order from the facts. In the systematic knowledge of the world thus arising the concept of causality rules. When it determines experience one-sidedly, there is no room for the concepts of value and purpose. In the view of reality the physical world is then so preponderant in scope and power, that the units of mental life appear as mere interpolations in the text of this world. Furthermore, only the mathematical and experimental knowledge of the physical world has the means to reach the goal of the cognitive attitude. Hence, this explanation of the world interprets the mental realm as derived from the physical. And when the critical standpoint shows the phenomenal character of the physical world, naturalism and materialism become the positivism based on natural science. Or the *Weltanschauung* is determined by the attitude of the emotional life. It is concerned with the values of things, the values of life, the meaning and sense of the world. The whole of outer reality then appears as the expression of something inner, and so it is taken as the unfolding of an unconsciously or consciously active mind. Accordingly, in each of the many, divided, restricted, individual agents this standpoint reveals an immanent divine element, which determines phenomena with the purposiveness to be found in consciousness. Thus objective idealism, panentheism, or pantheism originates. But if the volitional attitude governs the view of the world, then we see the schema of the mind as independent of nature, or as transcendent. The projection of this upon the universe forms the concepts of divine personality, of creation, and of the sovereignty of personality over against the course of nature.

In the sphere of objective awareness each of these *Weltanschauungen* combines knowledge of the world, evaluation of life, and principles of action. Their power lies in their inner unification of personality in its various activities. And their thoughtful grasp of ambiguous life through one of our general attitudes and its laws gives each of them attractive force and the possibility of logical development.

3. *The Insolubility of the Problem. The Decline of the Power of Metaphysics*

Metaphysics has spread out in an immeasurable wealth of forms. It goes restlessly forward from possibility to possibility. Satisfied with no form, it changes each into a new one. A hidden contradiction in its very essence crops out again in each of its creations, forcing it to drop the given form and look for another. For metaphysics has a remarkable duality. It aims to solve the riddle of the world and of life, and it aims to be universally valid. One face it turns to religion and poetry, the other to the particular sciences. Metaphysics is, itself, neither a science in the sense of these sciences, nor is it art or religion. From the start it presupposes that in the mystery of life there is a point accessible to rigorous thinking. If this point exists, as Aristotle, Spinoza, Hegel, and Schopenhauer assumed, then philosophy is more than any religion or any art, and even more than the particular sciences. Where shall we strike this point, at which conceptual knowledge and its object, the world-riddle, are united, and at which this singular world-order not only allows us to perceive particular regularities of occurrence, but becomes intelligible in its essence? It must lie beyond the field of the particular sciences and beyond their methods. Metaphysics must rise above the reflections of the understanding to find its own object and its own method. The metaphysical attempts at this have been surveyed and their inadequacy indicated. We are not to review here the reasons, developed since Voltaire, Hume, and Kant, which explain the continual change of metaphysical systems and their inability to satisfy the demands of science. I am selecting only what is relevant to the plan before us.

The causal knowledge of reality; the feeling of value, meaning, and significance; the volitional attitude containing within itself the goal of conduct and the principle of obligation: these are various general attitudes, combined in the structure of mind. Their mental relation is revealed to us in lived experience; it is one of the ultimate facts of consciousness within reach of introspection. The subject has these various attitudes toward objects; one cannot go back behind this fact to a reason for it. So the categories of being, cause, value, and purpose, originating as they do in these attitudes, can be reduced neither to one another nor to a higher principle. We can comprehend the world by only one of the basic categories. We can never perceive, as it were, more than one side of our relation to it, never the whole relation as it would be defined by the systematic unity of these categories. This is the first reason for the impossibility of metaphysics: to succeed it must always either unite the categories sophistically or distort the content of our consciousness. A further limitation of conceptual thinking appears within each of these attitudes. (1) We can think back to no ultimate, unconditioned cause of the conditioned system of events. For the ordering of a multiplicity, whose elements are uniformly related to one another, remains itself a riddle, and from the changeless One neither change nor plurality can be conceptually derived. (2) We can never overcome the subjective and relative character of evaluations, which stems from their origin in feeling. An unconditioned value is a postulate, but not a realizable concept. (3) We cannot point out a highest or unconditioned purpose, since this presupposes the establishment of an unconditional value, and the universally valid principle of action which is contained in mutual obligation does not permit one to deduce the purposes of the individual or of society.

But although no metaphysics can satisfy the demands for scientific proof, philosophy still has a sound position in studying the relation of the mind to the world, each general attitude expressing an aspect of this world. Philosophy is not able to grasp the world in its essence through a metaphysical system, demonstrated with universal validity. But every serious poem discloses a feature of life, never before seen in this light, and poetry thus reveals to us the various sides of life in ever new products. No work of art contains the whole view, and yet we approach it by means of them all. Likewise in the typical *Weltanschauungen* of philosophy a world confronts us, as it appears when a powerful philosophical personality makes one of the general attitudes toward the world dominant over the others, and its categories over theirs. So from the vast labor of the metaphysical mind the historical consciousness remains, repeating this labor in itself and thus coming to know the unfathomable depth of the world. The last word of the mind which has surveyed all these *Weltanschauungen* is not the relativity of each but the sovereignty of the mind over against every single one of them, and also the positive consciousness of how in the various attitudes of the mind the one reality of the world exists for us.

It is the task of the theory of *Weltanschauungen* so to analyze the historical development of the religious attitude, poetry, and metaphysics, in opposition to relativism, as to present systematically the relation of the human mind to the riddle of the world and of life.

IV. PHILOSOPHY AND SCIENCE

In the conceptual and demonstrative work of metaphysics reflection on thought itself, on its forms and its laws, grows steadily. The conditions of knowledge are investigated: the assumption that a reality exists independently of us and our thinking can reach it; the belief that persons exist beyond us and we can understand them; and finally the presupposition that the temporal course of our inner state is real, and that lived experiences, as they are projected in introspection, can be correctly represented in thought. Reflection on the processes in which a *Weltanschauung* arises, and on the grounds which justify its presuppositions, accompanies its formation and grows steadily in the conflict of metaphysical systems.

And at the same time the innermost nature of the philosophical *Weltanschauung* determines its relation to human culture and its purposive systems. Culture has been organized for us according to the inner relations between knowledge of the world, life and affective experience, and the field of practical affairs, where our practical ideals are realized. The structural system of mind is expressed in this cultural pattern and also determines the philosophical *Weltanschauung*, which thus becomes related to all sides of culture. And as this *Weltanschauung* strives for universal validity and everywhere seeks logical foundation and coherence, it must make itself felt in all spheres of culture, raising to consciousness what occurs there, grounding, criticizing, and combining. But here it is confronted by the reflection which has arisen in the purposive systems of culture itself.

1. *The Functions of Philosophy which Arise from Conceptual Activity in Cultural Life*

Not only in the *Weltanschauung* has man's reflection on his conduct and aspiration to universally valid knowledge developed. Before philosophers appeared, the separation of the functions of the state and the classification of constitutions had resulted from political activity. In the conduct of legal actions and transactions the basic concepts of criminal and civil law had evolved. The religions had formulated dogmas, distinct from one another, yet interrelated. Artistic techniques had been distinguished. For every advance of human purposive systems to more complex forms occurs under the guidance of conceptual thought.

Thus functions of philosophy develop which carry further the thinking done in the several fields of culture. As no fixed boundary separates religious from philosophical metaphysics, so also technical thinking grows continuously into philosophical. Everywhere the philosophical mind is characterized by universal introspection and the character-building and reforming power rooted in it, and at the same time by the strong tendency to logical foundation and coherence. Such a function of philosophy is not necessarily committed to the formation of a *Weltanschauung*, and it persists even where metaphysics is not sought or not admitted.

2. The General Doctrine of Knowledge and Theory concerning the Particular Fields of Culture

So the character of philosophy as reflection of the mind on itself produces its other aspect, which has always persisted along with the striving for a universally valid *Weltanschauung*. In the *Weltanschauung* the experience growing out of our general attitudes is gathered into an objective unity. But when these attitudes themselves in relation to their contents become objects of consciousness, when the experience arising in these attitudes is tested and validated, then the other side of self-reflection appears. Regarded from this side, philosophy is the basic science which studies the form, principle, and coherence of all thought-processes seeking valid knowledge. As logic, it investigates the conditions under which reasoning is self-evidently valid (and, of course, in every field in which thought-processes appear). As epistemology it goes back from the consciousness of the reality of the lived experience and the objective givenness of the outer percept to the justifications of these presuppositions of our knowledge. As such a theory of knowledge it is science.

This, the most important function of philosophy, relates it to the various spheres of culture, and in each of them it undertakes tasks of a special kind.

In the sphere of cosmic speculation and knowledge philosophy enters into relation with the particular sciences, which yield the parts of that knowledge. This function most clearly involves logic and epistemology as the basic work of philosophy. It clarifies the methods of the particular sciences by means of general logic. With this logic it connects the methodological concepts which have originated in these sciences. It looks for the presuppositions, goals, and limits of natural scientific knowledge, and it applies the results thus obtained to the problems of inner structure and mutual bearings in the two great groups: the natural sciences and the human studies. None of its relations to any other cultural system is so clear and intelligible; none has developed so harmoniously. And thus, even among the one-sided definitions of philosophy there is none which would be so evident as that it is the theory of theories, the logical grounding and combining of the particular sciences for knowledge of reality.

Less transparent is the relation of philosophy to experience of life. Life is the inner relation of mental activities in the system of the person. Experience of life is the growing meditation and reflection on life. It raises the relative, subjective, accidental, and separate elements in the rudimentary forms of purposive action to the insight into what is valuable and fitting for us. What do the passions mean in the whole economy of our life? What worth has sacrifice in a natural life, or honor and outward recognition? But the answers to such questions are sought not only in the individual's experience of life; this experience broadens to that which society achieves. Society is the comprehensive regulator of the life of feeling and impulse. In law and custom it restrains the unruly passions, as the common life requires. Through division of labor, marriage, and property it creates conditions for the orderly satisfaction of the impulses, thus freeing men from their dreadful tyranny. Life wins room for the higher feelings and aspirations, and these can gain predominance. The experience of life which society acquires in such achievements leads to ever truer appraisals of life's values, and through public opinion gives them a secure, regulated position. Thus out of itself society generates a scale of values, which then influences the individual. On this social basis personal experience of life now arises in many ways from lived experience of value as its primary material, and makes itself felt. Other lessons we learn as we witness the passions of men—emotions which ruin them and hence their relations to others, their consequent sufferings. And we supplement these personal experiences of life through history, which shows human destiny writ large, and through poetry. This above all reveals the painfully sweet stress of passion, its illusion and its dissolution. All things work together to make man freer and ready for resignation and the joy of surrender to the great objectivities of life.

Although this experience of life is haphazard at first, in becoming aware of the range and limits of its activity it must rise to an orderly reflection which strives to overcome the subjective character of evaluation. So it passes over into philosophy. All the stages along this way contain writings on character, temperament, the values and conduct of life. And as poetry is an important factor in developing the theory of all that, so this reading in the souls of men, this private appraisal of the values of things, again arouses an insatiable desire to understand, and thus leads to a clearer comprehension of the meaning of life. Homer is the teacher of reflective authors, and Euripides is their pupil. On the same basis every personally won religious attitude develops. Experiences of life, an awful penetration of insight into the illusion involved in all worldly values, commit every religious genius to the transcendent world. The religious experience would be empty and flat, if over against the felt misery, baseness, or at least pettiness of human affairs, the separations with the suffering entailed, elevation to holiness did not occur, as it were, like a release from this corruptible sphere. That road into solitude Buddha, Lao-tse, and (as some passages of the Gospels reveal) Christ also have taken. Augustine and Pascal have travelled it. And along with the sciences and social institutions of history experiences of life are the real foundation of philosophy, the basis of the personal element in the greatest philosophers. Their purification and justification is an essential and actually the most important part of philosophical systems. This is particularly clear in Plato, the Stoics, Spinoza, and indeed to a lesser extent also in Kant, for one who compares his *Anthropology* and his earlier writings. So now the system of values intrinsic to life and the system of objective, instrumental values arise in philosophy, the former belonging to a mental state, the latter to an external object which can produce those life-values.

Finally, in the context of cultural history philosophy has a relation to the practical world, its ideals and its institutions. For philosophy reflects on the will, its precepts, purposes, and goods. This will has been expressed in the institutions of business, law, government, technology, and morality; so only in them can the nature of the volitional attitude be clarified. As the relationship of purpose, obligation, and precept pervades them all, the deepest problem of philosophy in this field results: the great question, whether every moral law is deducible from purposes. The insight to which Kant rose in his categorical imperative can be developed into the proposition that in the moral world there is only one thing absolutely fixed, namely, that mutual obligation, in explicit agreement or in tacit assumption that the mutuality will stand, is unconditionally valid for every consciousness. Hence integrity, uprightness, fidelity, and honesty form the fixed frame of the moral world. Within it all purposes and all precepts of life, even goodness and the striving for fulfillment, are ordered in a hierarchy of obligations, which descends from strict duties to the moral requirement of goodness and sacrifice for others, and thence to the demand for self-realization. In establishing the region of authority for moral ideals, and in distinguishing the obligatory aspect of duty from the instability of purposes, the philosophical analysis of the moral consciousness determines the conditions under which the purposive systems within society develop. Philosophy, then, explains the actual social institutions, as the human studies describe and analyze them, by reference to the structure of the individual and of society. And from their teleological character philosophy derives their development and formative laws, although subordinating all these necessities to that highest law of obligation. Thus philosophy becomes an inner force, working toward the elevation of man and the progressive development of the social order, but at the same time furnishing fixed standards for these in the moral law and the inner realities of life.

At this point let us look back once more at the philosophical *Weltanschauung*. Here for the first time the whole breadth of its foundation can be surveyed. We catch the significance of experience of life for the development of a world-view. And finally we see how the great fields, marked out by the kinds of mental attitude, contain problems of importance in their own right, which can be treated quite independently of their place in the *Weltanschauung*.

So the relations of philosophy to the various fields of human life give it the right not only to ground and to combine the knowledge about these fields, and the particular sciences in which this knowledge has been organized, but also in philosophical disciplines like philosophy of law, philosophy of religion, and philosophy of art to rework the same fields. Beyond question, every one of these theories must be drawn from the historical and social situations which constitute the fields of art or religion, of law or government, and to this extent the work of philosophy coincides with that of the particular sciences. It is also clear that any such philosophical theory which, instead of drawing from the material itself, depends upon what is furnished in these sciences, perhaps checking this only here and there, has no right to exist. But, human ability being restricted, only in rare exceptions will the special investigator have so sure a mastery of logic, epistemology, and psychology that the philosophical theory would not contribute something new from these very fields. In any case, however, such separate philosophical theory is justified only as something provisional, arising from the insufficiencies of the present situation. On the other hand, the task of investigating the necessary relations of the sciences to one another, on which the logical constitution of each depends, will always remain an important function of philosophy.

3. *The Philosophical Spirit in the Sciences and in Literature*

The influence of metaphysics is steadily waning. On the other hand, philosophy is growing steadily more important in its function of grounding and connecting the thinking which has arisen in the particular fields of culture. The positivistic philosophy of d'Alembert, Comte, Mill, and Mach is significant in that it grows precisely out of an occupation with the particular sciences from within, follows their method, and always applies the standard of their universally valid knowledge. In another field the philosophical thinking of Carlyle or Nietzsche is positive in its very effort to generalize and to confirm the policies contained in experience of life and worked out by the poets and the prose-authors on the conduct of life. It is natural, then, that in this informal way philosophy is influencing more and more the whole mental life of modern times. The spirit of method, generalization, and inter-scientific connection, dominant in the natural science of Galileo, Kepler, and Newton, was then supported by the positivistic tendency of d'Alembert and Lagrange in permeating French natural science, and it continued its influence, on the basis of natural science and Kantian Criticism, in Ernst von Baer, Robert Mayer, Helmholtz, and Hertz. And this same philosophic spirit has come to the fore especially since the great socialistic theorists in the particular sciences of society and history. So it is characteristic of the present situation in philosophy that its strongest influences emanate not from the systems, but from this free philosophical thinking, which pervades the sciences and all literature. For even in the field of letters authors like Tolstoy and Maeterlinck exert an important philosophical influence. The drama, the novel, and now also lyric poetry have become vehicles of the most vital philosophical activity.

The philosophical spirit is present wherever a thinker, free from the fashion of a philosophical system, examines what appears to be odd and obscure in man, like instinct, authority, or faith. It is present wherever investigators with a consciousness of method regress from their science to its ultimate grounds of justification or press forward to generalizations which connect and confirm several sciences. It is present wherever values of life and ideals are reëxamined. What appears anywhere in chaotic or hostile struggle within an age or the heart of a man is to be reconciled through thought; what is obscure is to be clarified; what stands there in bare juxtaposition is to be mediated and connected. This spirit leaves no feeling of value and no striving in its immediacy, no precept and no knowledge in its isolation. For every valid thing it seeks the ground of its validity. In this sense the eighteenth century rightly called itself the philosophical century in virtue of its effective rule of reason over the dark, unconscious, instinctive forces within us and the regress from every historical product to its origin and its right.

V. The Concept of the Essence of Philosophy. A View of Its History and Structure

Philosophy has proved to be a group of very diverse functions, which, through insight into their regular connection, are collectively regarded as the essence of philosophy. A function always refers to a purposive system, and consists of a group of related activities which occur within this systematic whole. The concept is not derived from the analogy of organic life, nor does it refer to a faculty or an original ability. The functions of philosophy are related to the purposive structure both of the philosopher and of society. They are activities in which the person turns in upon himself and at the same time produces outward effects. In this they are akin to the activities of religion and of poetry. So philosophy is an activity which springs from the need of the individual mind for reflection on its behavior, for inner pattern and security of action, for a fixed form of its relation to the whole of human society. And philosophy is at the same time a function rooted in the structure of society and requisite for the completeness of social life. Accordingly, philosophy is a function which occurs uniformly in many persons and unites them in a social and historical continuum. In this latter sense it is a cultural system. For the characteristics of such a system are: uniformity of the activity in each individual member of the system, and solidarity of the individuals in whom this activity takes place. If this solidarity assumes fixed forms, organizations arise in the cultural system. Among all purposive systems those of art and of philosophy bind the individuals together least, for the function which the artist or the philosopher performs is dependent on no institutional forms of life. In this realm there is the highest freedom of the mind. The membership of the philosopher in such organizations as a university or an academy may increase his contribution to society. Nevertheless his permanent principle of life is the freedom of his thought, which must never be infringed, and which is indispensable not only for his philosophical character but also for the confidence in his absolute sincerity, and thus for his influence.

The most general characteristic, which belongs to all functions of philosophy, is rooted in the nature of objective awareness and conceptual thought. So regarded, philosophy appears as only the most consistent, vigorous, and comprehensive thinking, and it is separated from the empirical consciousness by no fixed boundary. From the form of conceptual thinking it follows that judging advances to highest generalizations, the forming and classifying of concepts to a conceptual architectonic with a highest apex; relating proceeds to an all-comprehensive system, and grounding to an ultimate principle. In this activity thinking refers to the common object of all the thinking acts of various persons, the systematic unity of sense-perception: the world. To form this world the plurality of things is ordered in space, and the variety of their changes and movements in time. All feelings and volitional acts of this world are arranged, through the definite location of the bodies belonging to them and the perceptual elements woven into them. All values, purposes, and goods, posited in these feelings or volitional acts, are fitted into it. Human life is embraced by it. And now thinking strives to express and to unite the whole content of perceptions, lived experiences, values, and purposes, as it is lived and given in the empirical consciousness (experience and the sciences of experience). In so doing thinking moves from the concatenation of things and of changes in the world toward a world-concept. For a ground it regresses to a world-principle, a world-cause. It seeks to determine the value, sense, and meaning of the world, and it asks for a world-purpose. Wherever this procedure of generalizing, of integrating, and of logical grounding is borne on by the cognitive drive and frees itself from the particular need and the limited interest, it passes over into philosophy. And wherever the subject, who relates himself to this world in his activity, rises in the same way to reflection on this activity of his, the reflection is philosophical. Accordingly, the fundamental characteristic in all functions of philosophy is the drive of the mind which transcends attachment to the determinate, finite, limited interest and strives to fit into some inclusive, definitive idea every theory which has arisen from a restricted need. This drive of thought springs from its rationality, and meets needs of human nature which well nigh defy reliable analysis: the joy in knowledge, ultimate security in relation to the world, the endeavor to release life from its restricted conditions. Every mental attitude seeks a fixed point, free from relativity.

This general function of philosophy is expressed, under the various conditions of historical life, in all the philosophical activities which we have surveyed. Particular functions of great vitality arise from these differing conditions: the development of a *Weltanschauung* to universal validity; the reflection of knowing on itself; the relation of theories, formed in the particular purposive systems, to the system of all knowledge; a culturally pervasive spirit of criticism, of universal synthesis, and of grounding in principle. They all prove to be particular activities which are rooted in the unitary essence of philosophy. For philosophy adapts itself to every stage in the development of culture and to all conditions determining its historical situation. And so we understand the continual change of its activities, the flexibility and mobility with which it now unfolds to the breadth of a system, now focuses its whole force effectively on a single problem, and is ever shifting its working energy to new tasks.

We have reached the point at which the presentation of the essence of philosophy illuminates its history in retrospect and clarifies its systematic unity as we look ahead. This history would be understood: (1) if the coherence of the functions of philosophy were to explain the order in which, under the conditions of culture, the problems appear, together and successively, and their possible solutions are considered in turn; (2) if the progressive reflection of knowing upon itself were described in its chief stages; (3) if the history studied how the theories, arising in the purposive systems of culture, are related by the comprehensive philosophical spirit to the systematic unity of knowledge, and hence further developed; how philosophy creates new disciplines in the human studies and then transfers these disciplines to the particular sciences; and (4) if it showed how from the state of consciousness of an era and from national traits one can gain insight into the particular forms which the philosophical *Weltanschauungen* assume, and yet at the same time into the steady advance of the great types of these *Weltanschauungen*. So then, the history of philosophy leaves a legacy to systematic philosophical labor: the three problems of laying a foundation for the particular sciences, establishing them on this foundation, and bringing them together; and the task of coming to final terms with the incessant need for ultimate reflection on being, ground, value, purpose, and their interconnection in the *Weltanschauung,* no matter in what form and direction this settlement takes place.

Index of Persons

A

Aeschylus, 53.
Albertus Magnus, 49, 50, 52.
Alembert, J. le R. d', 21, 62, 72.
Alexander the Great, 12.
Anaxagoras, 47.
Antony, Mark, 54.
Aquinas, St. Thomas, 47, 49, 52.
Aristotle, 7, 10, 11, 12, 27, 59, 65.
Augustine, St., 51, 70.
Avenarius, R. H. L., 63.

B

Bacon, Francis, 21.
Baer, K. E. von, 72.
Bain, Alexander, 23.
Beethoven, Ludwig van, 53.
Beneke, F. E., 23.
Bentham, Jeremy, 23.
Berkeley, George, 60.
Boehme, Jakob, 29.
Bruno, Giordano, 52, 59.
Brutus, Marcus Junius, 54.
Buddha, 70.

C

Caesar, Caius Julius, 54.
Calderón de la Barca, Pedro, 58.
Capella, Martianus, 21.
Carlyle, Thomas, 31, 63, 72.
Cassius Longinus, Gaius, 54.
Cervantes Saavedra, Miguel de, 59.
Christ, 28, 40, 49, 70.
Cicero, Marcus Tullius, 13, 63.
Clement of Alexandria, 28.
Comte, Auguste, 7, 21, 62, 63, 72.
Croesus, 9.

D

Dante Alighieri, 55, 58, 59.
Democritus, 7, 63.
Descartes, René, 7, 14, 15, 51, 52.
Diderot, Denis, 59.
Duns Scotus, John, 47.

E

Elizabeth, Queen of England, 55.
Emerson, R. W., 31.
Epictetus, 13.
Epicurus, 63.
Euripides, 59, 70.

F

Fechner, G. T., 16, 17.
Fichte, J. G., 7, 17, 19, 40, 62, 63.

G

Galileo, Galilei, 15, 72.
Goethe, J. W. von, 40, 53, 55, 57, 59, 63.
Grotius, Hugo, 12.

H

Haller, Albrecht von, 56.
Hegel, G. W. F., 7, 16, 17, 60, 62, 63, 65.
Helmholtz, H. L. F. von, 19, 72.
Henry the Fifth, King of England, 55.
Heraclitus, 9, 60, 63.
Herbart, J. F., 17, 23.
Herodotus, 8, 9.
Hertz, H. R., 72.
Hobbes, Thomas, 15, 21, 62, 63.
Hölderlin, J. C. F., 56.
Homer, 59, 70.
Hume, David, 7, 15, 16, 23, 65.

J

Justin Martyr, 28.

K

Kant, Immanuel, 7, 15, 16, 17, 19, 20, 40, 52, 59, 60, 62, 63, 65, 70.
Kepler, Johann, 72.

L

Lagrange, J. L., 72.
Lao-tse, 70.
Leibniz, G. W., 7, 15, 17, 27, 52, 60, 62, 63.
Lessing, G. E., 29, 30, 59.
Lipps, Theodor, 23, 24.
Locke, John, 7, 15, 16, 60.
Lotze, R. H., 16, 17.
Lucretius Carus, Titus, 13, 56, 63.

M

Mach, Ernst, 72.
Maeterlinck, Maurice, 31, 72.
Maine de Biran, M. F. P. G., 63.
Marcus Aurelius Antoninus, 13, 30, 31.
Mayer, J. R., 72.
Michelangelo Buonarroti, 53.
Mill, James, 23.
Mill, J. S., 23, 72.
Minucius Felix, Marcus, 28.
Molière (J. B. Poquelin), 59.
Montaigne, M. E. de, 31.

Montesquieu, Baron de la Brède et de, 12.

N

Newton, Sir Isaac, 72.
Nicholas of Cusa, 51-52.
Nietzsche, F. W., 31, 40, 72.

O

Origen, 28.

P

Pascal, Blaise, 70.
Plato, 7, 9, 10, 11, 12, 19, 27, 31, 63, 70.
Plutarch, 54, 55.
Porphyry, 28.
Proclus, 28.
Pythagoras, 8, 9, 27.

R

Racine, J. B., 59.
Raphael Santi, 40.
Rousseau, J. J., 40.
Ruskin, John, 31.

S

Schelling, F. W. J. von, 16, 17, 63.
Schiller, J. C. F., 40, 56, 58, 59.
Schlegel, A. W., 57.
Schlegel, Friedrich, 57.
Schleiermacher, F. D. E., 16, 17, 63.
Schopenhauer, Arthur, 16, 17, 31, 52, 65.
Seneca, Lucius Annaeus, 13.
Shaftesbury, Third Earl of, 63.
Shakespeare, William, 54, 59.
Smith, Adam, 23.
Socrates, 8, 9, 10.
Solon, 9.
Spinoza, Baruch, 7, 15, 52, 59, 62, 63, 65, 70.

T

Thales, 27.
Thucydides, 8, 9.
Tolstoy, Count L. N., 31, 72.
Turgot, A. R. J., 21.

V

Vincent of Beauvais, 21.
Voltaire (F. M. Arouet), 65.

X

Xenophon, 8.

Z

Zarathustra, 52.

www.ingramcontent.com/pod-product-compliance
Lightning Source LLC
Chambersburg PA
CBHW031644170426
43195CB00035B/571